Taft, Wilson,
and World Order

Taft, Wilson, and World Order

David H. Burton

Madison • Teaneck
Fairleigh Dickenson Press
London: Associated University Presses

©2003 by Rosemont Publishing & Printing Corp.

Associated University Presses
2010 Eastpark Boulevard
Cranbury, NJ 08512

Associated University Presses
16 Barter Street
London WC1A 2AH, England

Associated University Presses
P.O. Box 338, Port Credit
Mississauga, Ontario
Canada L5G 4L8

The paper used in this publication meets the requirements of the American National Standard for Permanence of Paper for Printed Library Materials Z39.48-1984.

Library of Congress Cataloging-in-Publication Data

Burton, David Henry, 1925-
    Taft, Wilson, and world order / by David H. Burton.
        p. cm.
    Includes bibliographical references and index.
    ISBN 0-8386-3969-0 (alk. paper)
    1. Taft, William H. (William Howard), 1857-1930—Views on peace. 2. Wilson, Woodrow, 1856-1924—Views on peace. 3. United States—Foreign relations—1909-1913. 4. United States—Foreign relations—1913-1921. 5. World politics—1900-1918. 6. League of Nations—History. 7. Presidents—United States—Biography. I. Title.

E762 .B88 2003
973.91'2'092—dc21

2002071287

PRINTED IN THE UNITED STATES OF AMERICA

FOR

MUCH ADMIRED COLLEAGUES
AND
FRIENDS OF LONG STANDING

Thomas Keefe	Thomas Marzik
Randall Miller	Raymond Schmandt
Phillip Smith	Katie Sibley

Contents

Preface

THIS IS A STUDY OF THE RELATIONSHIP AT A CRITICAL TIME IN TWENTIETH century history of two of the most farsighted statesmen of their generation. Born but a year apart, learned men, presidents of the United States, and apostles of world peace, they were similar but distinct in their public philosophies. Trained in the law and utterly devoted to it, Taft stood in contrast to Wilson who wrote widely about government and history in keeping with a university career. Their respective backgrounds and experiences in public service were the foundations upon which they built their proposals for peace amongst and between nations. At the time of their occupancy of the White House the great powers in the West were divided into rival camps. Immediately before 1914 and acting in their presidential capacity they had proposed treaties of arbitration between the United States and other nations. With the onset of World War I Taft and Wilson advanced their singular ideas along the lines of a league of nations, to be established once the war was over, in order to promote peace in the years to come. How their league conceptions differed and how they were similar in their objectives, what they did in public and in private to put in place an instrument to work for world order, and the reasons for their ultimate failure combine to identify the theme and the purpose of the study.

This account does not propose to compare and/or contrast the rationales of the two league advocates to the advantage of either Wilson or Taft. Its purpose, rather, is to demonstrate how each man arrived at his prescription for curing the ills besetting the international community. For Taft it was a question of law, backed by the military, lessons he had first learned while civil governor of the Philippines.

For Wilson international understandings were more a matter of morality. He preferred to rely on the goodwill of nations, which itself would be guided less by self-interest and more by the common bonds of humanity. In the thinking of Taft and Wilson alike, the time had come to end all wars but as the world has come to realize, that was not to be.

This book has come about from a growing awareness of the critical importance of William Howard Taft for an understanding of American politics, domestic and foreign, in the first decades of the last century. Despite a major Taft biography of the "life and times" variety in addition to significant monographs dealing with foreign policy, both pre-presidential and presidential, and a detailed treatment of his years as chief justice of the Supreme Court, Taft remains a less than imposing figure to students of early twentieth-century American history. Part of this may be due to his presidency, sandwiched between that of Theodore Roosevelt, the irrepressible Teddy, and Woodrow Wilson, the tragedian. Much has been written about the Roosevelt-Taft friendship and how and why it fell apart, and about Roosevelt and Wilson, for that matter. In turn, too little mind has been paid to Taft and Wilson as the shadows of war fell across their world.

That Taft and Wilson were learned men who helped to distinguish the presidential office in their time is well established. In large measure it was this learned turn of mind, based on education and wide reading, which led them to appreciate the place of international law in the making of a peaceful world. It would have been integral to their conduct of diplomacy, whether there had been a world war or not. And then the war was upon them.

Taft's studies at Yale, and particularly exposure to the scholarly writings of Theodore Dwight Woolsey, which took up both matters of international law and the role of government, "theoretically and practically," provided him with a solid grounding in some of the very areas occupying much of his career in public service. What better way to examine Taft's vision of world order than by placing his ideas alongside those of Woodrow Wilson. As an academician and scholar Wilson's range of study was wide and deep. He wrote warmly of the importance of great men in history, knowingly of the problems of governmental administration, and provocatively of congressional and constitutional rule. In the period 1909–1919 Taft and Wilson were separated more by party affiliation than by public philosophy. Despite their like-minded position on reform—Taft was more progressive than he has been made to appear and Wilson's convictions fell well short of the ultra-progressivism displayed by someone like Robert LaFollotte—it is their understanding of world order that invites examination. And the conclusion may be that at a critical moment for world peace, the summer of 1919, they spoke the will of the American people more honestly than did the United States Senate, which scuttled the Versailles Treaty and mocked the vision of the peacemakers of 1919.

My thanks to a number of colleagues who have aided and supported me in this study. James Dougherty's own writings as well as his advice profited me a great deal. Others helped by their interest and belief in the value of this undertaking, including Frank Gerrity, Thomas Marzik, Randall Miller, Elwyn Chase, Clarence Walton, John Monagan, Alec Campbell, and Esmond Wright. I find I am happily in their debt. The Drexel Library staff, and especially Mary Martinson and Chris Dixon, deserve special mention.

Taft, Wilson,
and World Order

Introduction

As World War I was grinding to a halt Woodrow Wilson took it upon himself to lay out a grand design for world order, which, if agreed to by the leading nations, promised global security. In keeping with the terminology he had used in his book, *The State*, published as long before as 1889, Wilson wrote of a "league of nations." Other leaders, no less dedicated than Wilson to international peace, were prepared to pursue what was considered a more realistic approach by means of a League to Enforce Peace. In the United States one of its most prominent spokesmen was ex-president William Howard Taft.

Taft and Wilson enjoyed a common inheritance based on history and political theory. The writings of Bodin, Grotius, and Vattel among many others had worked to shape the thinking of several generations of statesmen and to a lesser degree, the rulers they served. But there was a common set of values dating from antiquity, strengthened by Christianity, reformulated by the Enlightenment. This inheritance made for a code of behavior applicable in the first instance to individuals and ideally embraced by nations. Such had been the challenge since the emergence of nation-states, that these concentrations of political power must be led to see they were nothing more than individuals writ large. If nations were to avoid mutual destruction, the possibility of which became more and more apparent as weapons of mass annihilation matured in the direction of the ultimate weapon, peoples must learn to live together under a code of international law, with an agency at hand to make sure the laws were obeyed. Taft and Wilson were responsive in their own separate ways to this daunting responsibility, convinced, no doubt, of what they deemed the moral superiority of the United States ordained its mission of leadership.

The problem of world order, whether the term is applied to competing colonial empires from the sixteenth century onward or to the latter nineteenth/early twentieth centuries with their fiercely nationalistic rivalries, has been both an issue and a challenge to the sovereign states of the modern era. Political philosophers and practical-minded statesmen alike have wrestled with the proposals engendered by a search for an ordered world and they have resolved matters peacefully only on occasion and usually for brief periods of time. The United States, isolated as it was, or thought itself to be until World War I, paid little attention to the problem apart from the Monroe Doctrine, a kind of ordering of the Western Hemisphere, with American interests foremost. Yet more and more as global space was reduced in time and distance this posture could not be maintained. If the American empire was launched by President McKinley it was left to his immediate successors to rethink the nation's *weltpolitik*. Theodore Roosevelt's "world movement" frame of reference was never given formulation. It simply described and justified the spread of the advanced nations over the backward peoples and the waste spaces of the earth. In contrast, Presidents Taft and Wilson recognized the problem and the challenge as matters to be reckoned with by means of international cooperation, with the United States an active participant. World War I, to be sure, left the powers with a pressing need to provide a structure for maintaining international law and order, lest the catastrophe of the "Great War" be repeated by an even greater war. That the politicians and statesmen in 1918–19 failed mankind and the nation-state system may well underscore the intrinsic difficulty of achieving world order, as borne out by the history of the human race to the close of the second millennium.

As sobering as these thoughts are it is appropriate to point out that as the nineteenth century gave way to the twentieth hopes ran high, especially in the West, that a new dispensation was at hand. Establishment of the Courts of International Justice at The Hague promised both mediation and adjudication of differences between countries. The conference device, as used at Algeciras in 1905, and arbitration commissions, ad hoc in character or defined by treaty, also held out prospects for a more peaceful world. Presidents Taft and Wilson were cautiously optimistic in this regard. In each of their administrations arbitration by treaty agreement was much discussed if not successfully implemented, a sure sign they were committed to the use of good offices to resolve disputes between nations, their own among them.

Overtones of the biographical in this study render some comment appropriate. Every use of biography, if only in an ancillary way, encounters the fundamental question that can be particularized with reference to Taft and Wilson: Did the times shape these two quite different men or did the opposite occur? The answer must surely be that events were too sweeping in their effects for either Taft or Wilson to control them. Yet, somehow, the great man theory of history continues to attract and very nearly to persuade that a single man or woman by reason of work undertaken and completed can make an essential difference in the unfolding of events. Sidney Hook, when considering the place of the individual in history, wrote of the "hero" and went on to define the hero as an event-maker, the person who had made things happen in a particular way, or at a particular time, with intended results.

An often used method of treating historical figures is through the device of "life and times" of the biographical subject. In the case of Taft and Wilson the reverse of that design, namely the "times and life" may prove more fruitful. This latter technique deserves attention, especially when it comes to Taft and Wilson and world order. At what juncture in their respective careers did they become activists in the pursuit of peace by means of an international body? Did not their years of growth and maturation, well before they had achieved positions of public importance, alert them to the need for an international community, like-minded in its attitude toward the waste of war and the value of peace? That prospect was real enough, the more so because wars between the sovereign powers of the Old World had been few and limited ones, counting from 1815 and the Congress of Vienna. Foolish optimists might well believe that great wars were a thing of the past, but neither Taft nor Wilson saw things that way. Why else would they have pursued so doggedly arbitration treaties among the great powers? When World War I broke out they were in agreement their country could not turn its back on Europe and the world. But how to mediate a struggle fueled by nationalistic passions that celebrated the death of men. And once the war was over, due perhaps to mutual exhaustion, the perplexing solution to an ending of all wars became uppermost in their thinking. Yet the design of the machinery to guarantee world peace tended to divide them. How could this be? One of the purposes of this study is to account for the differences and to ask if these were no more than distinctions that could have been reconciled had not politics, combined with personal ambition, so polluted the air as to render compromise impractical and thereby impossible.

1

A Common Inheritance

Wᴵʟʟᴵᴀᴍ Hᴏᴡᴀʀᴅ Tᴀꜰᴛ ᴀɴᴅ Wᴏᴏᴅʀᴏᴡ Wᴵʟꜱᴏɴ ᴇɴᴊᴏʏᴇᴅ ᴀ ᴄᴏᴍᴍᴏɴ inheritance regarding the life of the mind in the broad sense. Equally important, their understanding of and their devotion to law as a means of advancing civilization within and among nations derived from common sources. Taft, of course, was very much the lawyer by training and by temperament so that whatever situation he encountered in his life of public service, law in constitution, law in statute, law in treaty, appealed to him as both a first and last resort. Wilson's ways of thinking and judging also had something of a legal aura about them. His writings on history and government make this evident. As students at Yale and Princeton the two studied much the same history from ancient to modern times. Each was influenced, for example, by the writings of Theodore Dwight Woolsey, the Yale professor, who introduced them to the theory and practice of international law from reading his classic study, *International Law*.[1] They also came to recognize his authority in his *Political Science* with its warnings against the excesses of democracy, all the while advocating the rule of law.[2] This is but an odd coincidence, yet it speaks to that common inheritance, the history of ideas and the impact of ideas on that vast collection of people and events portraying the face and form of civilization in the West.

From the inception of western civilization, attempts have been made by men and by societies to establish forms of political organization, an ordering of efforts, aimed at peace and prosperity. Peace might well involve conquests and prosperity for some, bought at the expense of others. What is important to stress is the natural instinct to bring order out of confusion in the first instance because of the impulse to survive, and that attained, the will to choose those means thought best suited to satisfy all other needs common to human kind. Hence the place of philosophies, systems of religion and law, and the interplay of the particulars of each. Beginning with the Greek city-states, Roman uses of law, and the monotheism of the Hebrews there was a fusion, however deliberated, that slowly moved civilization in the West in the direction of nation state, achieved only at the midpoint of the second millennium of the common era. Once the phenomenon of the nation-state was fixed in place the wisdom of the Greeks, the Roman genius for ordering, and the inspiration of the Christian spirit came together prompting efforts to promote order among various and sometimes mutually hostile peoples. The growth of a law of nations was gradual. As Taft and Wilson came of age the concept had taken on a reality as there continued to be uncertainty about its workability. International peace through law was an ideal each in his own way came to embrace.

There is evidence of cooperation between the Greek city-states, limited in nature, but indicative of a recognition of the need to define the rules of warfare and even a restricted form of arbitration. The Aetolian and Achaean leagues represent early organized efforts toward cooperation and collective action against aggressors. In contrast, the Romans saw no purpose to develop law or practice along such lines. By definition the Empire was "international" and therefore law unto itself. In one particular, settling disputes between conquered provinces, the office of *praetor peregrines* was created but that came down to nothing more than orders from the capital.[3] In the Middle Ages the greatest of thinkers, Thomas Aquinas (1225–74) gave some attention to the secular state in his writings; he saw no need, however, to stress unity of peoples or among princedoms. Their common-faith belief was enough.[4] As the Age of Faith retreated before a rising Humanism, Dante (1265–1321) was moved to speculate about worldly political matters. In his study, *De Monarchia*, part medieval and part humanistic, he argued that "mankind is part of a universal system of which God is the comptroller," an assertion nicely balanced by the observation: "Mankind is best off when most are free." Dante pined for a restoration of the old empire, the glories of Rome revisited, with a monarch who would rule "in conformity with laws common to all and lead it in the direction of peace."[5] Such were portions of the inheritance Taft and Wilson were willed from the history and thought of the premodern era.

The emergence of the nation-state system in western Europe constituted a sea of change in politics, domestic and foreign. Nations now claimed sovereignty, the ultimate allegiance of the people, of whatever rank, was due secular authority. From 1500 onward Western man and his worldly activities ever more surely replaced God as the measure of all things. Ironically, clerics were among the first commentators to discuss the reality of the law of nations, the starting point of a recognizable form of international law. One of these thinkers was Vittoria (1486–1546), a Dominican mendicant, and another, Suarez (1548–1617), a Jesuit priest. But in the long run it was the secular mind and orientation that prevailed: Bodin (1530–96), Machiavelli (1469–1527), and Gentilis (1556–1608). Although a divine element was not totally absent, God retreated step by step from the center of man's concern. A reading of Suarez, for example, reveals an almost otherworldly quality, as when he wrote of the universal unity inhering in all nations and all races. His assumptions rested on a certain metaphysics alien to new ways of thinking in the modern era.[6] Gentilis, a jurist who one day would be Regius Professor of Law at Oxford, was far more secular in his views. In his best known book, *De Juri Belli*, he anticipated much that became familiar in international law as it developed. He deduced the rules of law not from metaphysical sources but from the practices of states and the writings of historians. In his discussion of war Gentilis showed concern about the brutality of war and sought ways to mitigate the baleful effects based on human rather than legal grounds. Furthermore, he identified suggestions for terms of formal treaties of peace proposing such was crucial in enabling states to reach agreement to end hostilities with honor.[7]

One writer Taft and Wilson were persuaded by was Hugo Grotius (1583–1645), often referred to as "the father of international law." Grotius was motivated by a love of justice and of humanity, stressing these values in all his writings and especially in his magnum opus, *De Juri Belli Ac Pacis*. The laws of war and peace dictated if men were thought of as belonging to different nations this did not relieve leaders from all control in matters of justice and humaneness. Such findings were based on the law of right reason. Thus any action taken must be consonant with man's natural and social condition. Grotius also advanced the doctrine of all nations as being equal and independent according to their mores and their histories. Still another feature of his canon of international law was the concept of extraterritoriality and freedom of the high seas in time of war. Hugo Grotius's advocacy of principles of international law did indeed point in the direction of rules of peace and war as practiced by nations centuries later. His judgments, it should be stressed, were in no small measure based on personal observations of the brutality of warfare in his time, and not merely principles developed in the closet. It is interesting to note that Woolsey in *International Law* makes pointed reference to Grotius, ignoring the likes of Vittoria and Suarez, not out of ignorance but, perhaps, because of their historical associations.[8]

Two powerful forces were at work as the sixteenth century unfolded. One was capitalism with its already established methods centered on property and profits. These had surfaced as the distinguishing elements of the new economy in the late Renaissance. With the discovery of the New World and a rediscovery of the East, capitalism literally exploded. Trade with the Indies, east and west, trade wherever profit could be turned—be it in precious metals, luxury items in textiles and food, or slaves—came to dominate the economic life of the nations along the Atlantic seaboard: Spain, Portugal, France, England, and Holland. By attaining economic self-sufficiency their political independence was virtually guaranteed, supported by military and naval power. The term mercantilism may be applied, *mutatis mutandi*, to the commercial outlook of all trading nations, albeit some practiced it more successfully than others. Sources of wealth had to be guarded against the designs of rival nations, which all too quickly made for dangerous rivalries as nations clashed at home and abroad.

The onset of the same century, or to be precise, 1517, witnessed the start of the Protestant Reformation, which in due time produced the Catholic Counter-Reformation. Although the Age of Faith had apparently succumbed to the blandishments of the Renaissance humanism by no means did religion suffer an immediate demise. To the contrary, for upward of 150 years the kingdoms of Europe, now clearly identified as Protestant or Catholic, warred with each other over issues of piety and profit. Religion became one of the surefire ways to measure a nation and its people in as much as all the nations were monarchies and all sought wealth. Religion was therefore the distinguishing mark, Catholic princes fighting Protestant princes as a matter of rite and right. Churches became instruments of the state. Henry VIII led the way in England and the German princes rallied in defense and protection of Luther so that his movement quickly became a symbol of aspiring German nationhood. On the other hand, the Gallican Church in France, still tethered to Rome in matters of faith and morals, was under the thumb of the king. Paris was indeed worth a Mass. The religion of the prince became the religion of the people, either out of conviction or compromise of conscience. This identification of state and church endured well into the time of William Howard Taft and Woodrow Wilson. America conceived of itself as a Protestant stronghold, Wilson was a strict Calvinist, the offspring of two generations of clergymen. For his part Taft refused to allow himself to be considered for the presidency of Yale University because he was not a believing Christian (he professed Unitarianism), which he deemed a necessary qualification for the headship of his alma mater.

If, as asserted by Gentilis, the rule of law between nations should be based on the practices of states, it took the Thirty Years War to bring about acceptance of his teaching. The war began over issues of religion as Protestants and Catholics continued to resort to arms to settle territorial and other disputes, and as Calvinists insisted they too had equal rights of confession in areas largely Lutheran. The peace ending the war was, however, more a matter of settling rival political and dynastic ambitions. Meanwhile, three decades of brutal warfare had seen death and destruction almost beyond measure. The methods employed were appalling and, accompanied by plague and pestilence, villages and villagers alike were wiped out. In the settlement, the Peace of Westphalia, the concept of the nation-state as the vital force in western Europe was recognized as firmly in place. Grotius witnessed the unspeakable terror visited on the populace and was to protest in the name of justice and humanity, which cannot be unduly stressed. Though dead by the time the peace was finalized his writings both reflected and influenced new thinking about law governing the behavior of nations toward one another. Each prince was seen to possess sovereign authority within his own domains, free to make war or peace and to enter into treaties. A sovereignty might be as large as France or as small as the bishopric of Metz but in theory, all entities were equal, possessed of the right to exist independently. Westphalia has been termed the first modern peace conference. In sessions from 1645 to 1648 stipulations were agreed upon which transferred jurisdictions, enlarged duchies, and confirmed ruling houses. The geopolitical map of Europe was determined for decades to come. War had not been done away with but example had been given whereby it was deemed honorable to end hostilities for the sake of suffering humanity. In *International Law* Woolsey took note of the Thirty Years War pointing out that at times opposing generals entered into conventions to give and receive quarter, a harbinger perhaps of a more humane warfare. Ever the eager students, Taft and Wilson likely studied such particulars in Woolsey's book as he explained how custom hardened into law.[9]

The acceptance of the practices sanctioned by the Peace of Westphalia was slow in coming in the years down to the Peace of Utrecht (1714) ending the War of the Spanish Succession. Out of these new wars emerged a new concept promising to preserve international peace: the idea of balance of power. If no one nation were allowed to grow so strong as to threaten or to act against another sovereign state then peace would prevail, again in theory. In actuality this very argument could be used to justify attacking a neighboring nation in order to maintain balance of power. Nonetheless "balance of power" became an idée fixe in the minds of European statesmen.

Of Grotius's successors who wrote treatises on matters pertaining to international law two men especially should be singled out. Vattel (1714–67) discussed primary rights and duties of states and Lampredi (1732–93) advanced the principle of armed neutrality as one of the rights of nations.[10] Related to this was the doctrine of freedom of the seas, the rules of search and seizure, and of blockade and contraband. All these were of increasing importance by the late eighteenth century. True, most of the seafaring nations had their own set of practices so there were inconsistencies between them often leading to misunderstandings. What Lampredi intended was to point to a resolution in a way seemingly fair to all parties. The wars of the French Revolution and Napoleon put great strain on the observance of the most basic rules. Woodrow Wilson in *A History of the American People* showed himself fully cognizant of the dangers implicit in conflicting enforcements as registered in the undeclared war with France, 1797–98 and actions on the high seas leading in to the War of 1812. And in his lifetime, during the Civil War, the incident involving the British mail steamer Trent, the operation of the Union blockade, and the actions taken by the Confederate raiders all brought the dangers growing out of the principles associated with Lampredi's name into sharp relief. The lesson conveyed was the pressing need to clarify, and perhaps to attempt to codify the law of the sea.

Out of the titanic struggle engulfing Europe from 1793 to 1815 came a remarkable effort to actualize international accord so roundly abused in the previous decades. The Congress of Vienna meeting in 1814–15 and attended by representatives of the major powers, including France where monarchy had been restored, sired the Holy Alliance. It was a meeting of minds on the part of Austria, Russia, and Prussia. More importantly it also saw the birth of the concert of Europe as France and Great Britain joined in a plan to stabilize the nation-state system. It became a matter of mutual regard, a prelude to mutual trust and cooperation. The Congress formalized international diplomacy, set forth a number of principles including denunciation of the African slave trade. If the Holy Alliance was a fantasy indulged in by Czar Alexander I the concert of Europe constituted a practical method for keeping the peace by and among nations.[11]

The ideas of the French Revolution, combined with the code Napoleon, had cast down seeds of future upheavals wherever French armies had penetrated. Post-Napoleonic revolutionary movements sprung up in Spain, Portugal, Naples, and Piedmont. The powers, save Great Britain, assembled in congress at Troppau in 1818 determined to use force to maintain the monarchical status quo. Two years later the Congress of Verona, with England again standing down, resolved as far as possible to attempt to aid Spain as it sought to recover its breakaway colonies in the New World. Both Britain and the United States, for different but complementary motives, pointedly opposed such adventuring. It was at this juncture that President Monroe enunciated the doctrine bearing his name. The British accepted the doctrine insofar as it suited their large policy for the western hemisphere but did not consider it part of international law. This became abundantly clear years later, in 1895, at the time of the Anglo-American dispute over the boundary line of Venezuela. President Cleveland stated forcefully that the Monroe Doctrine was part of international law and Lord Salisbury just as forcefully rejected this contention. No doubt Taft and Wilson followed this diplomatic controversy inasmuch as the affair appeared for a time to threaten war. And surely they were happy to see a peaceful settlement.

For the remainder of the nineteenth century, and virtually to the onset of the First World War recognition of the worth and workability of international law grew apace. In 1856, at the conclusion of the Crimean War, the powers met and signed the Declaration of Paris, which set forth the rules of sea warfare, including the abolition of privateers, stating a neutral flag guaranteed neutral goods except for contraband, and that a blockade to be so recognized had to be effective and therefore more than a paper declaration. Incidentally, Woolsey commented approvingly on these rules of maritime warfare as a further indication of the progress being made in the law of nations.

By far the most important convention of the last half of the nineteenth century was signed in 1864 in Geneva creating the International Red Cross. Because wars, at least limited in scope but brutal for all of that, continued to break out—the Austro-Prussian War, the Franco-Prussian War, the Spanish-American War, and the Boer War —the place and the value of the Red Cross became generally accepted. The Geneva Convention sought to regulate the treatment of prisoners of war, to aid the wounded, and to speak out, as never before done, for humanitarian concerns. And it was heard. Most all of the European nations signed the Convention, but the United States held back. The Franco-Prussian War was the first occasion the Red Cross had to attempt its work of amelioration and it performed reasonably well considering the novelty of its role. The American Civil War heroine, Clara Barton, in Europe at the time, had not heard of the Red Cross before. Upon returning home she was determined to persuade her government to join the Red Cross. It took nearly fifteen years of lobbying Congress and three presidents before the United States became a signatory to the Convention of 1864. Because of the respect the International Red Cross had won almost at once some people took this as an augury that war itself might give way to peaceful arbitration of even the most serious disagreements between nations.

This sentiment was expressed in a meaningful way with the convening of the First Hague Conference in 1899. What did these promising meetings achieve? Not very much. Despite the initial optimism informing its sessions the overall results were disappointing. Military minds tended to dominate the discussions, none moreso than that of the United States delegate, A. T. Mahan. He had a reputation as an advocate of a powerful American navy so that talk of disarmament and the avoidance of an arms race fell flat. In short, powerful nations would keep the peace. But some resolutions aimed at international accord were adopted: specification of procedures for the settlement of disputes, the principles of the Geneva Convention made applicable to naval warfare, and an early attempt to codify some of the customs and practices of armies that had recently evolved. A Second Hague Conference met in 1907. Forward-looking resolutions were again passed. A convention with regard to laying submarine mines, one dealing with the conversion of merchantmen to war ships, a third referring to the creation of prize courts were typical of the business taken up. Very much work remained, but the movement toward the willingness of nations to put some strictures on the conduct of war was to some extent encouraging.

Coinciding with the prospect that modern war, if not preventable, could be moderated in its worst aspects, was a renewed interest in the work of the American Peace Movement. It had had a life of its own since 1815 when Peace Societies were formed in Massachusetts and in New York. Their leaders and members alike had a long history of a advocating understanding between nations. Dozens of towns and cities could boast of their support for the ideals of the Peace Movement. In some instances at least their influence was limited by their identification as pacifists, which in nineteenth century America carried a negative meaning. Yet it must be said the original and abiding purpose of the Peace Movement was to work for peace through negotiation and arbitration. Andrew Carnegie, the robber baron turned philanthropist, added to the momentum of the Peace Movement with a gift of ten million dollars to further its aims.

The Hague Conferences, agitation by spokesmen for the Peace Movement, and the munificent outlay of money by Carnegie could but put pressure on the world powers. Only the governments themselves, however, were in a position to make dreams of peace come true. In the United States presidents from McKinley to Wilson had spoken out in favor of arbitration, either under terms of a treaty or by ad hoc arrangement. The sticking point invariably was the unwillingness of the Senate to agree to terms. There were countless meetings, conferences, discussions, and rallies by peace advocates during the fifty years before the outbreak of World War I with too little to show for these various efforts. As disappointed as President Taft was at the rejection by the Senate of the proposed arbitration treaties with Great Britain and France, when rendered meaningless by Senatorial amendments in 1911 President Wilson had a still more bitter experience. Treaties of arbitration watered down by the Senate were passed into law shortly before war was declared in 1914. The cries for peace were drowned out by the guns of August as rivalry between national alliances threatened to bring an end to Western civilization.[12]

2
Taft in Action

WILLIAM HOWARD TAFT HELD THREE COMMAND POSITIONS BETWEEN 1900 and 1913. As first civil governor of the Philippines he was responsible for taking the initial steps in the preparation of the Filipino people for self-rule while at the same time the islands were undergoing "pacification." In 1904 Theodore Roosevelt named him Secretary of War, a position giving Taft unusual leverage in his trouble-shooting missions in Tokyo and Havana where he acted as the president's anointed representative. And as with every occupant of the White House Taft was commander-in-chief from 1909–13. In his book, *The President and His Powers*, written in 1916, he argued that a president should be as strong as the law allowed. An advocate of Dollar Diplomacy, Taft practiced what he preached even if that meant acting like a commanding officer, when he judged the situation required it. In each of these administrative posts he was motivated by a deep and abiding desire to maintain order under law. An examination of his actions as civil governor, cabinet member, and president will underscore he was intent on getting peaceful resolutions of major issues, yet prepared to mix force, or threat of force, or the appearance of the threat of force to achieve his objective. This ongoing experience for a period of a dozen successive years made Taft a realist when handling affairs of state without abandoning the workable ideal of order under law.[1]

Acquisition and occupation of the Philippine Islands by the United States was the least predictable outcome of the Spanish-American War. It was logical, however, that the United States would want to take and hold the Islands as a base in the far Pacific. The forces at work propelling the nation to the status of a world power had become increasingly evident all through the 1890s. The closing of the continental frontier logically suggested the attraction of a trans-Pacific extension of the frontier. The lure of the China trade captivated businessmen and expansionists alike. Competition among the powers for access to markets and raw materials in China was acute. Yet the United States had neither leaseholds nor extraterritorial privileges on the mainland. A Far Eastern outpost became an imperative. The Philippines were close enough to China to enable Washington to exert political influence and at the same time develop commercial contacts. Such ambitions could not be realized without the presence of land and naval forces nearby. In international affairs the 1890s were a time of testing among the great powers, of maneuvering for strategic advantage among nations, of enlarging empires, whether in Asia, Africa, or possibly even in the Americas. It was logical therefore, given the opportunities presented by the outcome of the Spanish-American War, not only in the Caribbean Basin as the peculiar preserve of American dollar diplomacy to be practiced by President Taft, but to see the Philippines as the great entrepôt for Far Eastern trade.

If any explanation beyond political and economic advancement is required to justify American imperialism, the tenets of Social Darwinism were conveniently at hand. This doctrine had a pronounced appeal to Americans, a people who had struggled to get ahead, to conquer a continent with an abundance of natural resources to be exploited. Undoubtedly it had helped to produce an American sense of superiority regarding other nations and peoples. As they had proven themselves by bringing vast areas of North America under their sway it seemed entirely plausible to them they had a right, nay a duty, to continue their conquests. This was especially so because wherever they had settled they had established self-governing communities. Possession of lands near at hand or far away carried with it the responsibility to promote the welfare of the native races through law and self-rule. This feeling of obligation, which few Americans sympathized with more keenly than William Howard Taft, added an important element of righteousness, cleansing American imperialism of its grosser impurities by imparting to it a moral purpose.

The long-term occupation of the Philippine Islands was, in consequence, a logical outcome of these complex forces. Yet the United States had not formulated a "large policy" either before or after the defeat of the Spanish fleet at the battle of Manila. The landing of American troops, ably abetted by Filipino irregulars, longtime opponents of Spanish rule in the islands, made short work of the Spanish garrisons. Filipino leaders were convinced that with the foreign masters gone they would be free and independent. They were fully aware that the American declaration of war against Spain included a self-denying clause, the Teller Amendment, stating the United States had no intention of maintaining its hold on Cuba once order had been established. The war had been fought to free Cuba, not to conquer it. If the victors had no desire to take Cuba, an island ninety miles from the American mainland, it was logical to assume that the Philippines, nine thousand miles distant from America, would be treated in much the same fashion.

Logic was to give way to reality, however. Reluctant to enter upon war in April of 1898 President McKinley became a convinced imperialist with the passing months. The "splendid little war" ended on a totally triumphant note: Cuba was to be a client state, Puerto Rico, a dependency, and the Philippines, a colony. Cuba and Puerto Rico presented no immediate problem but the decision to retain a Far Eastern possession was a different matter. As sound, or at least as defensible, as McKinley's reasons for taking the whole of the archipelago, the president and his advisors failed to see much beyond the moment. If the standard formula of American continental expansion was to be applied, the obstacles were formidable, if not insurmountable. Could viable self-government be established by and for such a people, unschooled as they were. McKinley proudly announced the purpose of occupation was to: "civilize, sanitize and Christianize [sic]" the islanders in preparation, not for statehood but for nationhood, some years hence. It was a breathtaking proposition but how could it succeed? Americans knew little or nothing about the history, the culture, the ways of this people. The task McKinley had set for the nation would begin from minus-zero even if there had been no independence movement. As were the Cubans, the Filipinos had been yearning and striving for years to be free of Spanish control. Having aided United States troops in the taking of Manila, leaders of the irregulars were confident that a free Cuba guaranteed a free Philippines. By the beginning of 1899, however, war between the two armies had broken out. Not only the island soldiers but much of the population came to look upon the McKinley policy as betrayal.[2]

This proved not to be a "splendid little war." Far from it. The United States had to muster 70,000 men to pacify the archipelago, and it took well over two years to complete the task. As the Filipinos had no regular army they resorted to guerrilla tactics, always difficult for rank and file soldiers to deal with. The Army officer corps displayed nothing but contempt for their enemy and the common soldiers mirrored the view of their superiors. The Filipinos were, in a word, a lesser breed without the law. But if Kipling's phrase is appropriate it must be added McKinley was prepared to take up the white man's burden.

The president wanted an end to the violence of insurrection, which the generals argued could be achieved only by the application of *force majeure*. Meanwhile, McKinley, acting on his own instincts, organized a commission of prominent civilians to visit the Islands, study the total situation, get to know the leaders, mostly the great landowners and other men of education. They were to make recommendations with a view to seeking an accommodation between American presence and Filipino prospects. Named the Schurman Commission after its chairman, Jacob Gould Schurman, president of Cornell University, a careful, thorough, and encouraging report was in McKinley's hands by late 1899. It called for a civil governor whose responsibility it would be to move the islanders in the direction of self-rule.[3]

Perhaps it should be argued that the Filipinos knew and understood the Americans as little as they were understood. To them they had simply traded one imperialist master for another. McKinley's hopes and Schurman's recommendations did not necessarily ring true to a people long subjugated. And there was a broader issue, peculiarly American. Would American ideals of republican government become so badly tarnished by colonialism as to force a withdrawal from the Philippines on principle, thereby giving in to local demands for independence? The anti-imperialists of 1898 were to make this argument when McKinley stood for re-election in 1900. Until the American electorate had its say the struggle between U.S. regulars and Filipino guerrillas would go on. Despite their best efforts the anti-imperialists failed to make the 1900 presidential race a single issue election. Filipino hopes were sobered by McKinley's victory over William Jennings Bryan.

With fighting at many locations in the island group building in intensity President McKinley made perhaps his most adroit move in seeking and finding the man who would serve as first civil governor.[4]

In January, 1900, well before election time, the president called William Howard Taft to Washington and offered him a position on a second commission from which would emerge a civilian administration to govern the Philippines. At the time Taft was serving as a federal appeals judge in Cincinnati. Under the impression he was being summoned to the White House to discuss appointment to the Supreme Court (it appears that Justice Horace Gray was in failing health) Taft was taken aback altogether when asked to assume the Philippines assignment, and possibly, as president of the commission, to be named the first civil governor. The task at hand would be to prepare the people there for taking up the responsibilities of self-government in keeping with the recommendations of the Schurman Commission. Not attuned to the developing United States Far Eastern foreign policy Taft was in fact unsympathetic to the whole idea of an American presence in the Philippines. As he informed McKinley he "deprecated our taking the Philippines because of the assumption of a burden by us contrary to our traditions. . . . But being there we must exert ourselves to construct a government which would be adopted to the needs of the people so that they might develop into a self-governing community." His was an ambivalence shared by many of his countrymen.[5]

William Howard Taft was a man of peace and no doubt discouraged by news from the Philippines describing the vicious warfare in progress. Did he want to be a party to that kind of enterprise: on the other hand was the use of maximum force the only way to proceed? As long as there was active, organized resistance to the very presence of the United States the war, tragically, must go on. After much soul searching and some assurance that one day he might win an appointment to the Supreme Court in recognition of helping to bring orderly government to the Philippines, Taft accepted the president's offer. It carried with it the built-in understanding he would head up the commission and at the appropriate time be named civil governor. What worried Taft the most as he, his wife and three children made their way across the Pacific, was the war being so bitterly waged by both sides. He was expected to be able to bring order under law and peace to a suffering people. But the war, at a distance, appeared unwinable by either side: a frightening prospect.

When Taft arrived in Manila in early June, 1900, what was the military situation, and what was the state of mind of the indigenous population and that of the American soldiery? Beginning in January, 1899, the United States came down hard on both the military and civilian elements who stood for independence. General Elwell Otis commanded the United States regiments and his approach to "pacification" was simple and without mercy: kill and burn, kill as many resisters as possible and burn their villages to the ground, scorch the earth. In one encounter, which may serve to exemplify Otis's overall approach, the town of Tititia was literally wiped out at the general's command. Upward of one thousand men, women and children were executed and their houses burned to the ground in retaliation for the death of one American soldier killed in the vicinity of Tititia. So far out of control was American behavior—Otis encouraged his troopers to kill at will—he was relieved of his command. Once back in the United States he boasted that it was this kind of assault that had broken the back of the insurgency at a time when it was far from being subdued. The war continued for eighteen months after Otis had left the islands. General Arthur MacArthur came on as military governor in May, 1900, just prior to Taft's arrival in Manila. His first official act was to declare a general amnesty—"complete amnesty for the past and liberty for the future." Taft must have found this reassuring, a welcome sign of a new way to pacification. If he believed there was to be harmony between general and civilian he was badly mistaken. A more practical-minded soldier than his predecessor, MacArthur nonetheless looked over a giant divide between newcomer and veteran. In short, the general held himself to be in charge, and the civilian commission a nuisance, however well intentioned. Taft, fresh from Washington, had the support of President McKinley and Secretary of War Root, more than sufficient counterweight to MacArthur's pretensions. The administration was determined to install civil rule, which was to become abundantly clear over the next year. Where MacArthur found need to apply continued force Taft sought out opportunities to extend the olive branch. What the realities required was somewhere in between. Or to put it another way, use of firepower exclusively would likely have caused the fighting to continue indefinitely. Yet some military pressure was called for to give Taft's pragmatic approach time to be judged on its merits. Once the local leadership came to trust Taft's promises of steady steps in the direction of quasi-independence, and these were apparent almost at once, ongoing warfare lost its momentum. The carrot and the stick—the carrot was real and the stick continued to sting—proved a workable combination. The leader of the insurgent forces, Emilio Aguinaldo, came down from the hills in the spring of 1901 and signed an oath of allegiance, signaling that the end of fighting was in sight, even though meaningful pacification was not achieved until the next year.[6]

What Taft was able to do was to balance his distaste for the military embodied in the attitude and actions of General MacArthur with his responsibility to govern according to the Constitution and the law. Within a week of being on site Taft wrote his brother, Charles, to this effect: "The army is a necessary evil, it is not an agent to encourage the establishment of a well ordered civil government."[7] He was ready to take on both MacArthur and the brutality that, from the beginning, had defined military operations. Perhaps the basic difference between the two antagonists went deeper than their civilian-military roles. By nature Taft was a peace loving optimist, MacArthur a pessimist, if not a misanthrope. The General's mode was that of a conqueror whereas Taft deemed conquest a matter of appealing to the best interests of the Filipino people, replacing fear with hope.

Despite or because of the ongoing war, Taft acted quickly to set up an administrative system in order to deal with a wide variety of governmental responsibilities. These included land ownership disputes, construction of schools and roads, tax collection, legal codes, sanitation, and health care. In sum he recognized the need to provide for the day by day lives of the people. Under the Cooper Act, which he had helped to draft, Taft's authority was virtually without limit. He had in mind a simple form of government that, once in place, would acquaint the islanders with the basics of self-rule, namely, responsibilities always accompany freedom. And Taft was determined to introduce educated Filipinos into the scheme of things. Critics and doubters of this policy, with General MacArthur prominent among them, continued to protest as Taft continued to build. His vision of the future rested largely on his confidence in the ability of the Filipinos to mature politically. He believed it possible that as early as 1904 a semi-independent government could be in place. In the event it was 1907 before the first all-Filipino Congress was to meet, but meet it did. Much more than incidental to the reforms as they came into play was the governor's acceptance of Filipinos as social equals. The military were totally unsympathetic, but the people more and more convinced by such signs of goodwill that the Americans intended to help them even as they occupied their country.

The army, nonetheless, continued to have an important and very likely an indispensable part in the whole American undertaking. In fulfilling its main task of seeing to it that Taft's healing methods were allowed to go forward die-hard insurgents had to be kept at bay. Too often this meant taking casualties, few or many depending on the encounter. The most costly of these occurred in September, 1901, some weeks after Taft had been formally installed as civil governor and more than a year after the initiation of reform measures. At Samar a company of the 9th Infantry was ambushed with a loss of fifty eight men dead and others wounded. Fortunately this did not set off a series of encounters, as was at first feared, yet the threat to law and order was ever present. Taft was alarmed by what had happened at Samar, which occurred at just about the time news of McKinley's assassination reached Manila. The president had been an ardent supporter of Taft's work: it now fell to Secretary of War Root to explain to the new president, Theodore Roosevelt, particulars of American policy in the Islands. Roosevelt hardly needed to be persuaded that what Taft had done was the proper course to pursue, referring to the governor as the first great American proconsul.[8]

What then were the lessons regarding law and order William Howard Taft was to take away from his Philippine experience? Certainly he rejected the principle that force was the ultimate ratio in conducting affairs of state, the sort of proposition appealing to the thinking of men like A. T. Mahan or Theodore Roosevelt. But he would hardly have subscribed to Woodrow Wilson's judgment that public opinion should determine when force was unavoidable if legitimate objectives were to be realized. He was persuaded, rather, people must perceive that their best interests are involved both in the laws proposed for governance (something unlikely in the knee-jerk reaction of the military in the Philippine War) and in the breakdown of the political/social structure, which can not be allowed to come about. It is then, and only then, force by threat or in fact, may be called upon. Whether such a judgment was applicable in general was not for Taft open to question. True, some variations might have to be allowed but not at the risk of confusing means and ends. Justice must always be the objective of the legal system and actions when taken in pursuit of justice can not become the end itself. Killing Filipino insurgents was for Taft a painful means that he countenanced but only in limited measure, bearing always in mind the ultimate objective, peace and prosperity for America's wards.

The office of Secretary of War has rarely if ever been occupied by generals. On the contrary, from the early days of the Republic the cast of mind of the office holder had been civilian, save for Henry Knox in Washington's cabinet and Jefferson Davis, a West Pointer, under President Pierce. Down to Taft's time the most successful Secretary of War had been William Stanton who proved himself a master of logistical supply. But there was a war on during his tenure, and a civil war at that, the times calling for a man of his talents. A peace-loving man, Taft, as head of the War Department, saw no contradiction of purpose in answering Theodore Roosevelt's call to replace Elihu Root in 1904. It was a case of one complete civilian succeeding another.[9]

The War Department had served as a quasi-colonial office in the wake of the Spanish-American War. Secretary Root was an astute administrator for the newly acquired land: Puerto Rico, and the Philippines, along with the recently acquired Hawaiian Islands. He and Taft saw eye to eye on what was called for in the Philippines, the control of which was fraught with danger and challenge. Once he returned to Washington the new secretary could be counted on to continue to protect and promote Filipino interests. More pressing responsibilities came with the War Department job, however. In Panama, in Cuba, and in the Far East Taft was to become a troubleshooter for the president. In each of these areas of concern he demonstrated a knack for using the military or the threat thereof as he carried out the administration's policies. Relying on his Philippine experience he had come to know how to balance the use of force with an appeal to local self-interest so that order was maintained and peace realized.

As Secretary of War William Howard Taft was the senior American official directly responsible for overseeing the construction of the Panama Canal. The Republic of Panama was born in November, 1903, with the United States as midwife. By the terms of the Hay-Bunau-Varilla Treaty of that year a zone ten miles wide was ceded by Panama where the Canal was to be built. The prospects for a stable government in the tiny republic were not reassuring, a situation calling for vigilance by the United States once canal construction commenced. President Roosevelt delegated full power to Taft at the construction site. "All the work of the digging, construction and completion of the canal . . . shall be carried on or exercised under the supervision of the Secretary of War" read the executive order.[10] It was to be Taft and not Roosevelt who would "make the dirt fly" in Panama. Among the Secretary's many worries was the continued stability of the Panamanian government. And Taft did worry about what he described in private correspondence "the dirty, so-called republic." As he wrote his brother, Charles, in November, 1904 Panama was a "kind of Opera Bouffe republic and nation. Its army is not much larger than an army on an opera stage. We have four hundred marines and a fleet on one side and three naval vessels on the other" therefore the Panamanians had better behave. As for a revolution interrupting canal work Taft went on to say to his brother the Hay-Bunau-Varilla Treaty "permits us to prevent revolutions and I shall advise them we shall have no more."[11] The marked difference between Taft's attitude toward the Filipinos and the Panamanians is hard to ignore. In the Islands the Governor poured out his wrath on the generals, MacArthur at first and then his successor, General Adna Chaffee. Parental regard for the people in the Philippines was replaced by scorn for Latin Americans, or at least for the Central American countries. Wherein lies the explanation for this difference? Is it to be found in Lord Curzon's laconic phrase: "Taft was the first Saxon to love the Malay and the Malay returned it" rendering it a matter of chemistry? Were the Malay therefore exempted from negative evaluations associated with "the Black Legend," that anything derived from the south of Europe (Catholic Europe?) was suspect because it was corrupt? Did Taft have such presuppositions reenforced in dealings with Vatican officials pertinent to the Friars' Lands issue? Or was it that the Filipinos appeared to him as children who needed to be cared for, appealing to his fatherly instinct? Whatever the explanation, Taft kept up his guard as he proceeded to do a masterful job of making construction of the Panama Canal a reality.

According to the Platt Amendment, which had been added to a 1902 Army Appropriations bill, the United States agreed to bring to an end its military occupation of Cuba, dating from 1898, in return for Cuba amending its own constitution. Under the new arrangement Cuba was forbidden to alienate any of its territory to a foreign power or to become politically or financially dependent on another country. The Platt Amendment furthermore authorized the United States to intervene in Cuban affairs in order to maintain a stable government or to fulfill international obligations. From 1902 to 1906 no American forces were stationed there. A bitter struggle between moderates and liberals erupted, which threatened war in 1906. The threat became a reality in August when Tomas Palma was elected president and he proceeded to request American intervention to stave off bloodshed. President Roosevelt was reluctant to accede to the Palma request and is said to have muttered to himself he wished he could wipe Cuba off the map. What Roosevelt wanted to avoid was to give an instant response to Palma's plea, lest this become a recurring theme in Cuban-American relations. Yet he also had to bear in mind heavy American investments in the Cuban sugar industry would be at high risk if fighting broke out due to the absence of United States peacekeeping troops, should he fail to act.

The president decided to send Secretary of War Taft to Havana, instructing him to do everything possible to bring about "pacification," a term with more than a faint echo of times recently past in the Philippines. Before starting for Cuba Taft consulted with General J. Franklin Bell to ascertain the readiness of the army. He was informed a force of 6,000 could be assembled at once and an additional 18,000 could follow within the month. Taft was reassured, not knowing what he would find once in Havana. He wrote the president: "If we have to go in at all, I am in favor of going within with as much force as we can so as to end the business at once."[12] He could not have stated his willingness to involve the military more clearly.

Once in Cuba Taft made a quick assessment of the situation, deciding to announce the creation of a provisional government with himself as governor pro tempore but with full power. A contingent of United States troops also began to arrive. Taft judged the Cuban army too small and the rural guard too unreliable should fighting break out. The fact that American soldiers were on site was designed to forestall just that and no significant firefights ensued. Intervention had taken place even as the Roosevelt administration sought not to use the term. As the president wrote pointedly to the provisional governor: "Avoid the use of the word 'intervention' . . . and if possible place the landing of our sailors and marines on the grounds of conserving American interests."[13] But both Taft and Roosevelt knew full well troops were necessary if a stable government was to be reinstated and United States investments secured.

As events unfolded the role of the American military became central to the process of an emerging Cuban polity that would meet Taft's standards. Garrisons were established in the larger towns and troops also stood ready to assist the rural guards. They were there "as background to give confidence." And in consequence a calm settled in over the island. Taft was happy to leave Havana after a matter of days but the troops stayed on and on, down to 1909, by which time the Secretary of War had succeeded to the presidency. The troops in place might well be looked upon as part of the Taft legacy, a force "to give confidence." Resort to force was by degrees becoming part of the new president's thinking. Whether in the Philippines or Panama or Cuba, American interests, be they political or financial, had to be protected within these lands but also the lands had to be guarded against foreign encroachments. In keeping with the larger development of the United States as a world power Taft, consciously or not, was thinking in terms of *weltpolitik*. This is borne out more fully by a consideration of his part in the articulation of America's Far Eastern policy while he was secretary of war.

The decision by the United States to retain possession of the Philippine Islands over the long term rendered imperative a Far Eastern policy. In 1899 Secretary of State John Hay took the initial step by issuing the First Open Door Note. His object was to attempt to guarantee Sino-American trade by urging the powers having leaseholds in China to keep that country accessible to all nations choosing to have commercial relations there. Merchants and manufacturers, capital and capitalists alike should be welcomed for what they could bring to and take out of China. The note has been termed a piece of Yankee bluff since Hay was fully aware the powers already deeply committed to the exploitation of China and its resources were likely to pay it little heed. The point the secretary of state was making was that the United States was also in the hunt. A Second Open Door Note was issued the next year, 1900, one dramatically redefining American commitments in the Far East. Washington announced henceforth the United States would seek to protect the "territorial integrity" of China and that in the face of the possible reduction of the country to quasi-colonial status. Basic to this position the theory of balance of power as a means of maintaining order was now brought into practice. Balance of power as a technique had influenced the power politics of western Europe, a design to prevent domination by a single nation-state through an offsetting combination. This might be achieved by treaty or by response to a fear of conquest.

In the practical order the Roosevelt administration was worried that one power, or some set thereof, could emerge as the controlling agent of the China trade to the exclusion of the United States or other nations, and France comes to mind, having only a limited stake in the outcome. T. R. wisely recognized the most his country could do was to react to events as it sought to keep alive the spirit of the Open Door. The Russo-Japanese War (1904–06) was just such an event and Roosevelt moved adroitly in pursuing the dicta of balance of power. He was able to persuade both sides to the conflict, and for differing reasons, to come to the bargaining table, and on American soil, Portsmouth, New Hampshire. The upshot of the Treaty of Portsmouth was neither country attained total victory (or suffered total defeat) producing a balance of power from which the United States stood to benefit.

In the middle year of the conflict Roosevelt dispatched Secretary of War Taft to Tokyo, a significant detour from stated destination, Manila, there to visit with Filipino leaders. While in the Japanese capital Taft met with a number of high ranking imperial ministers. Talks centered on Japanese-American relations, present and future. One of Taft's concerns had to do with Tokyo's attitude toward an American controlled Philippines, always a sensitive matter with him because of his fondness for the people there. Discussing matters with the Japanese prime minister, Taro Katsura, these issues figured in the agenda: the Philippines, Korea, and balance of power in the Far East as a guarantor of peace. Two days of talks yielded a fruitful harvest. Tokyo disavowed any intention of meddling in the Philippines, Washington gave a green light to Japan in Korea—well, not exactly Washington but Secretary Taft acting on his own initiative. Finally the two nations along with Japan's formal ally, Great Britain, which by this date was an informal ally of the United States by reason of the "special relationship" now well advanced, would cooperate to keep order in the region. The resulting Taft-Katsura Agreement received the wholehearted approval of President Roosevelt, another feather in the administration's diplomatic cap.

What made the Japanese so amenable to the closing of ranks in the name of mutual self-interest? As a warrior nation where the samurai tradition was deeply bred in its culture Japan rightly appreciated Taft acting as the spokesman for the American commander-in-chief and in his own capacity as secretary of war. The Japanese were well aware that beginning in 1905 the president had successfully seen through the Congress legislation calling for a steady expansion of the United States Navy. The newest type warship, the dreadnought, was being added to the fleet. Roosevelt's purpose was to have a two ocean navy, one half of which would be stationed in the Pacific, at a base soon to be built at Pearl Harbor, Hawaii. No threat or even allusion to the use of force surfaced in the Taft-Katsura conversations, but the appearance of an increasingly armed and aggressive America could not have been lost on Katsura and his advisers. As for Taft, he was coming to know the ways of power politics and the role and function of balancing national interests in such a way as to achieve a viable relationship. The United States, literally over night, had become a major force in the Far East measured against the same standards by which the Japanese themselves had risen in war and peace. Both Tokyo and London concurred in this judgment.[14]

Diplomacy should never be pursued without consideration of the domestic side of the political coin. Two related issues were preoccupations at home in the United States, each having implications for Japanese-American accord. The segregation of Japanese children in the public schools of San Francisco and developing resentment against growing numbers of Japanese (among other Orientals) in the workforce were sources of discord. Taft readily recognized the offense given Nipponese amour propre as strong protests against discrimination were lodged by the embassy in Washington. Because the federal government had virtually no legal control relative to California schools the administration was put in an awkward position. Secretary Taft who planned to visit Manila to mark the first meeting of the Philippines Congress in 1907 was directed by the president to press on to Tokyo to mollify the Japanese. Taft was respected by the Japanese, but remained resentful of the treatment accorded their countrymen in America. Considerable attention in the talks was given to the possibility of war, rather much as a point of debate. For the first time since taking charge of the war department Taft found himself addressing war and its implications as he promoted peace. War between the two countries he pronounced "unthinkable" a proposition he stuck to throughout his mission. As he remarked in referring to the school segregation "there is nothing in these events of injustice" that "statesmen of honor and sanity" can not settle. He probably did not completely allay Tokyo's concerns. Be it remembered less than three months after Taft departed Japan, in October, 1907, Theodore Roosevelt's Great White Fleet steamed out of Hampton Roads, Virginia, for its worldwide voyage, a veritable preening of American naval power. Therefore it was Taft's purpose to reassure the Japanese in every way possible. As he announced in a major address before the Tokyo Chamber of Commerce "War between us would be a crime against modern civilization. It would be as wicked as it would be insane . . . an awful catastrophe." On a less flamboyant note it was implied such a conflict would run counter to the whole scheme of balance of power.[15] The progress of the Great White Fleet undoubtedly had a sobering effect on Japan. All in all Taft had carried out his assignment, smoothing the way for the Root-Takahira Agreement of 1908, which was based on a mutual understanding that peace, not war, was in the best interest of all. Taft assumed all along balance of power was the best way of keeping regional peace and prosperity.

During the Taft presidency American foreign policy remained focused on the Caribbean and the Far East. What distinguished it from Roosevelt's diplomacy was its emphasis on financial means to obtain desired results, a consideration of little concern theretofore. Unlike Roosevelt, Taft did not despise the "economic man" and quite naturally linked diplomacy to the promotion of United States business abroad. It became a matter of "dollar diplomacy." Whereas the president pushed his agenda in China, it lacked the strong political overtones of dollar diplomacy as practiced in Central America. There the worry persisted, as it had for some years past, of recurring political chaos carrying with it a threat to American-held property. This was sure to discourage further investments in the Dominican Republic, Nicaragua, and even Mexico. Political instability—revolutions were a too common occurrence—presented the Taft administration with occasions inviting "intervention" in domestic affairs of sovereign states, or to put it another way, to exercise police power in Central America lest mare nostrum turn into a Serbonian bog. And if intervention meant landing American marines and warships standing on the coast in support, President Taft, perhaps unenthusiastically, was prepared to do just that.

The model the administration proposed to imitate was laid down in the Dominican Republic years before, that is, to take over the troubled finances of a country in order to bring it back to a workable level of political life. This had in fact worked well for a number of years but with the assassination of the president by political enemies in 1911 the nation was again living under the shadow of impending chaos. Washington appeared to have little choice but to intervene in Dominican affairs once again. Two United States officials, William Doyle, chief of the Latin-American division at the State Department and Brigadier General Francis McIntyre, arrived in the island capital aboard the USS Prairie as 750 marines made their way ashore. But reestablishing sound government proved elusive. At one point Roman Catholic Archbishop Nouel served as president but the financial difficulties were unresolved. Loans from New York banks served as stopgaps for the remainder of Taft's time in office.[16]

The "show" of force in dealing with the Dominican Republic became the use of force with the onset of political unrest in Nicaragua. From 1909 to 1913 the president was never free of worry about conditions in that country. Regimes came and went, with the United States supporting this or that politician in hopes that American-owned property would be protected by the government in power. The disarray reached a flash point by 1912 when the president, Adolfo Diaz, was unable to give the necessary assurances as required by the State Department. Taft ordered in two thousand marines to restore order, and he offered no apology for taking military action. Marines remained in Nicaragua until 1925.[17]

The mixture of American property and Mexican politics prompted President Taft to speak out on his role as commander-in-chief as prescribed by the Constitution. In 1911 Mexico was on the verge of internal upheaval as one political faction struggled with another to take power. Mexican nationalism, as in the past, readily translated into anti-Americanism and understandably so, considering that 40 percent of the country's property was owned by United States controlled interests with only 35 percent in Mexican hands. As Taft put it: "we have two billions of American capital in Mexico that will be greatly endangered . . . were the government to go to pieces." When the crisis deepened the president ordered twenty thousand army troops to mobilize along the border and naval units were put on alert in the Gulf of Mexico. He was, in his own phrase, "within my province of commander-in-chief to order the army out for maneuvers; so I put that face on it." With no intention in interfering in internal Mexican affairs his mobilization order had a twofold purpose: to prevent the United States from becoming a source of arms supply for anti-government revolutionary forces and to underscore concern in Washington for the safety of American-owned property. As events turned uglier south of the border the president took the position, expressed privately, that he must protect "our people" as far as possible and their property by having the Mexican government understand "there is a God of Israel, and he is on duty."[18]

In each of the instances Taft advocated, approved, or allowed the use of military power and he did so for one reason, *viz.* to maintain internal order, as in the Philippines, or international order, by means of the operation of balance of power. In his policies as president these motives were fully evident even as, at the same time he was hard at work promoting dollar diplomacy. The two strands of purpose were intertwined. For the most part, and Japan is the obvious exception, he pressed for law and order for nations and peoples quite unprepared and therefore unable to achieve ordered societies by means of laws of their own devising. Thus order often had to be enforced as witnessed in what the United States with Taft as president on occasion undertook.

In dealings with what might be termed more advanced nations— those politically responsible, economically strong and willing to work in many circumstances at least for orchestrated international accord —Taft's approach was measured, idealistic and optimistic. Two such instances where he offered strong personal support in dealing with Congress stand out. First was a commercial treaty with Canada based on the principle of reciprocity. Admittedly there was no disquieting tension between the two neighbor nations. But the friendship could be deepened and regional peace more secure were the treaty to become law. The treaty, however, was rejected both by the United States Senate and that for local New England political reasons and by Canada where suspicions abounded that the treaty was aimed at undermining Canadian sovereignty.

Taft's reputation as a peace seeker was never more fully in evidence than in his proposed treaties of arbitration with Great Britain and France. He was extremely disappointed at the outcome, the failure of the United States Senate to approve not simply the treaties but the very idea behind them. In 1911 President Taft, directing the state department to draw up terms of the treaties, appears to have been caught up in the spirit of the day so well highlighted by the work of The Hague Tribunals. What Taft had in mind was a bedrock approach to arbitration between like-minded nations. There were to be no issues that were not justiciable. As he announced to a meeting of the American Arbitration and Peace League in 1912: "Personally I do not see anymore reason why matters of national honor should not be referred to a court of arbitration than matters of property or national proprietorship." It was a radical stand to take but he believed in it with all his heart. As he told Archie Butt, his military aide, the treaty "will be the great work of my administration. But just as it will be the greatest act during my four years it will also be my greatest failure if I do not get it ratified."[19] The Senate so eviscerated the terms of the two treaties the president would not forward them to London or Paris.

The reaction of the Senate, where Henry Cabot Lodge was a power on the Foreign Relations Committee, was strikingly prophetic of the fate of the Versailles Treaty some years later, enabling Taft to identify with Woodrow Wilson and his plight. But for now arbitration by treaty was dead and with it one of the last opportunities before World War I to exercise peaceful means of attaining international order. This is not to argue that had the treaties been in effect the 1914 war would have been avoided, after all the root causes of the conflict were European in origin. Nonetheless, they could well have proved a starting point for statesmen to build on in the future, which was basic in Taft's thinking.

3

Wilson in Contemplation

SCHOLARS STUDY, REFLECT ON, COMPARE, AND INTERPRET WHAT THEY FIND of interest to them and of importance to others. In short, they contemplate. Woodrow Wilson was such an individual, a scholar of repute and indeed a scholar for the greater part of his life. He once remarked he did not see himself as a scholar, referring to the sometime researchers who brought into print arcane and not overly useful findings of concern to the very few. Yet biographers and others who have written about him inevitably treat him as a scholar, a young scholar or mature scholar on one hand or viewing the whole of his life, a righteous scholar. To approach Woodrow Wilson as an American president who strove mightily to create a new world order in the aftermath of 1914–1918 his scholarship becomes central to understanding where he was coming from and why he was pointing the way to a permanent peace among nations. That there was more than scholarship shaping his political/diplomatic outlook whether as reform governor in New Jersey or Progressive president in Washington or as world leader must be taken into consideration. Wilson's abiding commitment to morality amongst nations no less than in individual relations is an ever-present feature of his conduct. And it is in his scholarly treatment of history past and in the making that his moral convictions can be more easily viewed and evaluated.

The future president's religious commitments were based on a foundation deeply laid. His father was a highly respected and influential Presbyterian divine. Each Sabbath day young Tommy listened to his father's finely crafted sermons; in Sunday school he mastered the catechism; every day he was made to feel the presence of the Lord. Looking back on his boyhood Wilson recalled "the atmospheric pressure of Christianity the week through." Yet in the teachings of Calvin no man was born to faith, he must freely accept it, finding God as a personal saviour through a religious experience or conversion. For Thomas Woodrow Wilson this occurred in the summer of 1873 when, after an intense period of introspection, he came to understand that God had elected him, a call he freely embraced. His father was a professor at the Presbyterian Theological Seminary in Columbia, South Carolina at the time and his son applied for full membership in the First Presbyterian Church of that city. He was now a saint. Years later when he was president Wilson returned to visit the chapel where he had prayed and had been converted, referring to it as "holy ground." For the purposes of this study it is his scholarly treatment of history past and history in the making where his moral convictions can be more easily viewed and evaluated.[1]

Three great historical events had a profound influence on Woodrow Wilson: the advent of Constitutional government for the American states 1787–89, the American Civil War 1861–1865, and World War I 1914–1918. All these milestones in the history of the United States directly and indirectly impacted on the president's thinking as he set his course to find an international order of peace growing out of mutual respect and trust. The first two events put down foundations which were firmly in place well before the outbreak of World War I: that conflict provided the opportunity, in fact the necessity, for Wilson, step by step from 1914 onwards, to fashion his grand design for a world made safe for democracy.

Wilson, the scholar, published in 1901 a five-volume account, *A History of the American People.*[2] By the standards of that day it was deemed a personal rendering of the nation's leaders and the men and women who followed them to achieve greatly. Of course he had to deal directly with that grouping of titans, the Founding Fathers. By replacing a confederation with a federated union they had established a model of how individual sovereignties could be brought together to govern and populate a continent. What seemed impossible to the higher political wisdom of the eighteenth century held out hope that twentieth century nations could be inspired to do likewise. Perhaps only an American could be brought to contemplate that, but by 1918 an American president appeared to have his hands on the levers of persuasion.

Above all other considerations the Civil War tested the durability of a "more perfect union." A Southerner, Wilson was never a champion of The Lost Cause. His interpretation of the outcome of the war is borne out both in *A History of the American People* and in an earlier work, *Division and Reunion* (1893), which covered the years 1829–77.[3] Wilson wrote plainly the survival of government under the Constitution was best for all sections of the country, intellectually consistent with the thrust of history as conceived by Whig historians, himself included. Victory had nonetheless been purchased at an enormously high price in lives and property. It had been a wrenching experience, North and South, prompting Lincoln—Wilson celebrated him as "the supreme American in our history"—to call for malice toward none, charity for all. Born in 1856 Wilson remembered the war through a child's eyes but he grew up in a South where the sacrifices made by the people had taken on mythic proportions. When later as president he said it was a terrible thing to lead this great nation into war the ghosts of the Civil War dead stood at his side. The psychological effects of the war when recalled in song and story produced in Wilson a respect for peace not only for America but for the world. If the bitterness of the Civil War could be moderated and lead on to a reconstituting of the Union then reconciliation as a rule common to humanity could always be invoked. The philosophy of the American Constitution melded with the emotional stirrings produced by victory and defeat within one nation making for elements in Woodrow Wilson's outlook, irrespective of World War I. But given that war the president was the more motivated and convinced world order could be established if peace without victory could be achieved.

From his days at The Johns Hopkins University in the 1880s until his departure from Princeton in 1908 Woodrow Wilson was absorbed in academic affairs, both scholarly and political. In other words there were few signs of a future public career, much less a preoccupation with world affairs. True, in his book, *The State* (1898), he made mention of "a league of nations" in a brief examination of international law.[4] In the larger context of the book this amounted to little more than a passing reference. It might be well to note that Wilson did not become a member of the American Peace Society until 1907. He joined to support the philosophy of the movement once he began to be concerned about the prospect of a major war growing out of the alliance system in place in Europe by that date. What is relevant to Wilsonian thinking from 1884 until 1907 must be distilled from a consideration of various writings and addresses that might deal with general issues; his article, "The Study of Administration," appearing in *Political Science Quarterly* in 1887 comes readily to mind.

Woodrow Wilson was a constitutionalist of the first order, which is to say, he had a touching faith in the power of the written word when it came to regulating the affairs of people. This commitment on his part reached the ultimate expression in the Covenant of the League of Nations. This does not mean he was disposed to hold that words alone could command behavior. Rather, once agreement had been reached on a single issue or regarding a form of government, what was written was written, and must be honored. Behind such a contention was the power of public opinion which in turn presupposed a democratic process, limited though it might be in its inclusiveness. It was central to the Whig interpretation of history. The progress which this posited could, with majority support by nations and peoples, federate the world. "World Federalism," to be sure, is more a mid-twentieth-century expression and the whipping boy of nation-state psychology. Wilson would have been sympathetic with it in the abstract but he was too much of a realist to think to put it into practice. Just as he insisted the states in the American union must retain their right to rule themselves in many particular ways, so the nations of the world must retain the distinctiveness of their political systems along with their culture in law and language. Wilson's league concept was confined to international relations as was the thinking of all the major advocates working in hopes of a new kind of world community.

Constitutions were central to Wilson's larger scholarly preoccupation, government and politics, and how these entwined and were interactive. A first book, *Congressional Government* (1885) and his last, *Constitutional Government* (1907) were assessments of how American government worked, and by indirection commentaries of government as such bear this out. Early in his career the aspiring professor published "The Study of Administration"[5] and "Character of Democracy" in *Atlantic Monthly* in 1889. Together, they are seminal in Wilson's thinking on world order as it developed over the years.

To Wilson, administration was neutral; it was as essential to a democratic republic as to a Napoleonic France. Getting done efficiently what the law called for was the heart of good administrative practice. Unfortunately, as experience so well demonstrated, America was not immune to the baleful influence of politics. "Administrative questions are not political questions," he insisted. The people did have a role to play; public opinion was the "authoritative critic" in the execution of administration. Wilson's real worry was too much public input, not too little. "Self-government does not consist in having a hand in everything," however much public opinion was useful to thwart domineering and illiberal officialdom. Wilson believed it was necessary to attack directly the widely held American conviction that as we were a people of political genius, administration would take care of itself. "Mere unschooled genius for affairs will not save us from blunders." It may be assumed from the stress the future chief executive placed on the study and practice of administration that he was beginning to move away from criticism of congressional government and heading toward an overall concern for responsive rule, which offered more constructive scholarly and practical prospects. The American challenge was all the more impressive because of the intricacies of the federal system of government and the need to synchronize the actions of the state and the national authorities. This consideration prompted Wilson to close his essay on a farsighted, almost prophetic note. He deserves to be quoted with the reminder that these sentences were set down in the late 1880s.

> If we solve this problem we shall again pilot the world. There is a tendency—is there not?—a tendency as yet dim, but already steadily impulsive and clearly destined to prevail, toward, first the confederation of parts of empires like the British, and finally of great states themselves. Instead of centralization of power, there is to be wide union with tolerated divisions of prerogative. This is a tendency towards the American type of governments joined with governments for the pursuit of common purposes, in honorary equality and honorable subordination. Like principles of civil liberty are everywhere fostering like methods of government; and if comparative studies of the ways and means of government should enable us to offer suggestions which will practically combine openness and vigor in the administration of such governments with ready docility to all serious, well-sustained public criticism, they will have proved themselves worthy to be ranked among the highest and most fruitful of the great departments of political study. That they will issue in such suggestions I confidently hope.

Wilson the scholar and the idealist were mutually supportive.[6]

Tied to his vision of international cooperation by sovereign states was the increase of democratic, or at least, more representative governments in the Western world. One of the great objectives of Wilson justifying entry into war in 1917 was "to make the world safe for democracy." In truth, only when enough of the world's polities were democratic could this dream begin to be realized. "The Character of Democracy in America"[7] despite its title was salient in this regard. The piece contained any number of the leading ideas of the day including those on science, inductive history, and socialism as a challenge to laissez-faire economic theory, the Teutonic origins of the common law, and, of course, a pronounced social Darwinism. The contentions were colored throughout by a concern for morality in public life; "politics was a sphere of moral action." "The Character of Democracy" was basically a historical inquiry, however, as it was from history that Wilson sought to extract a true philosophy of government. His study of the past underscored the evolution of legal and political institutions as they tended to progress toward a form of polity that was both representative and democratic. Democracy was the adult stage in political growth; when successful, it combined freedom with restraint. The foundation of democracy was moral because it comprised moral agents, the people. The people were crucial to its well-being. They must display the adult virtues, self-reliance and self-control, at the same time they enjoyed liberty and the freedom to choose. In so saying Wilson was arguing for, perhaps preaching is the better word, a synthesis of traditional values and scientific imperatives.

These articles published two years apart expressed key ingredients of an emerging conviction. The will of the people, that is, public opinion, when free to speak out will naturally, according to the Natural Law, seek accommodation in order to avoid conflict which could lead to war.

The State marked the coming of age of Woodrow Wilson as a political scientist, a book dealing with governments and government. In it was displayed a mastery of fact, fact being the raw material of inductive reasoning enabling him to offer insights and conclusions regarding Western political institutions. Questions were settled not by theory but by history, what history yielded to the observer. Of the many principles induced one in particular comes into play when nations deal with one another. Wilson conceded that all governments in their exercise of authority relied ultimately on force. By "force" he did not intend mere power, but the will of the few or the many or the community to realize its own purposes. In international affairs this could lead to competition and to conflict, given the character of international law at the close of the nineteenth century. Wilson summed up the situation in these words, full of hope and promise of a new day of peace and cooperation.

> International Law may be described as law in an incomplete state. It is law without a forceful sanction such as exists for the ordinary law of the land. There is no earthly power to which all nations are subject; there is no power, therefore, above the nations to enforce obedience to rules of conduct as between them, yet International Law is not lacking in sanction altogether; it rests upon those principles of right action, of justice, and of consideration which have so universal an acceptance in the moral judgment of men that they have been styled the Laws of Nature. Back of it in the first instance is the common public opinion of the world. When this public opinion is flouted, and the principles and practices of International Law are disregarded, then the physical force of individual states or groups of states may be brought to bear upon the law-breaker. International Law is the law of the international community of states; its principles are those upon which the successful life of that community depends. The society of states is not yet fully organized and International Law is incomplete just to the extent that this society lacks organization; its courts, its judges, its legislatures are rudimentary and are wanting as yet in that definiteness of constitution and authority which we find in individual states.[8]

After referencing writers like Grotius and Vattel and their appeals to the Law of Nature Wilson went on to take heart at the prospects for peace as he studied the history of Europe and the world since the Congress of Vienna. And he concluded "the formation of a league of nations to bring pressure to bear upon a state unmindful of its international obligations will go far towards supplying the sanction of regulated force which international law has hitherto lacked." As he wrote:

> These rules concern the conduct of war, diplomatic intercourse, the rights of citizens of one country living under the dominion of another, jurisdiction at sea, the rights and duties of neutrals, etc. Extradition principles are settled almost always by specific agreement between country and country, as are also commercial arrangements, fishing rights, and all similar matters not of universal bearing. But even in such matters example added to example is turning nations in the di-

rection of uniform principles; such, for instance, as that political of-
fences shall not be included among extraditable crimes, unless they
involve ordinary crimes of a very heinous nature, such as murder.[9]

Citing the various issues arising between nations, some of which had
sowed the seeds of past wars, Wilson had made a case, however pre-
liminarily, for his great future work.

In his study, *The State*, Wilson wrote as a student of government.
When taking up the most crucial era in the history of the republic in
Division and Reunion 1829–1889 (1893) his approach was a mix of
the governmental and historical, and in the end patriotically American. Looking ahead to his efforts to achieve world order comparisons
of federalism and confederalism, historically the Union and the Confederacy, as delineated *Division and Reunion* gave Wilson much food
for thought, once the scholar was transformed to the statesman. Wilson made no secret that he believed the outcome of the Civil War was
best for the people taken all in all.[10] He would later reiterate in his *A
History of the American People* (1903) a scholar's recognition that the
surrender of sovereignty by the several states was best for all the
people. Such action showed how a league of states was to become a
nation.[11] Nevertheless Wilson's examination in detail of provisions of
the Confederate constitution as well as its general character provide
specifics how states could agree on the means of achieving their
goals—freedom and prosperity—yet retain their identity as sovereignties. In proposing his "league of nations" Wilson understood
clearly that each member state "in its sovereign and independent
character"—the phrase he applied to states in the Confederacy—
would participate in league affairs for a common purpose, the very
state of affairs in the Confederacy. Indeed, the Montgomery constitution was more a forerunner of Wilson's league covenant than was the
Philadelphia constitution.[12] Just as the United States Constitution
went beyond theory to grow in practice so the League had the potential to do the same. Continuing to draw on *Division and Reunion* Wilson portrayed the centennial year, 1876, as marking the "Restoration
of Normal Conditions." "The national spirit was aroused and conscious now at last of its strength."[13] The point being stressed was of
course a national spirit that tended to guarantee success. In 1918–19
the emergence of an international "spirit" of cooperation was equally
central for Wilson's dream of a world made safe for democracy. He

was encouraged to believe this was possible to some extent at least by the ability of the American states and their peoples to make a fresh commitment to the nation after the bitterness of the Civil War and Reconstruction.

If the characterization of *A History of the American People* as a highly personalized version of its subject is apt, it seems entirely appropriate to determine how Wilson interpreted the framing of constitutional government following a period of virtual sovereignty by the thirteen states. He tended to emphasize the "spirit of the age." For example he thought it notable when the states with claims to vast tracts of land beyond their borders so easily conceded them to the control of Congress under the Articles of Confederation. Also part of that spirit was "the subtle, all pervasive uneasiness of the commercial enmity" between and among states. But such were the overarching conditions that a spirit of mutual trust at the political level was enough to prevail over the economic man and "render the constitution of a federal government adequate to the exigencies of the Union."[14]

When the convention met in Philadelphia in May of 1787 the feeling was not one of protest or disagreement but of the need to construct a government. Such a spirit included a sense of what should be done of "practical sagacity," of leadership, of knowledge, of government, and law. Perhaps it was not simply the contagion of the spirit of the age but a shaping of that spirit as well. The convention "had not passed measures to please but measures to save the country," according to Wilson.[15] Could not much the same be observed about the Fourteen Points, or more particularly about the Covenant of the League? In 1918–19 Wilson was influenced by his reading of early American history and motivated by the feeling he was justified in not seeking to please but to save the world.

In the years between leaving the presidency of Princeton and entering upon the presidency of the United States Woodrow Wilson was preoccupied with domestic politics and its many reform issues. A highly successful term as a progressive governor in New Jersey was followed by an intense presidential campaign with national, rather than international questions, in the fore. There was little enough need to take world affairs into account inasmuch as the electorate was itself indifferent to such matters. Once in the White House a myriad of challenges faced the new president, some of them diplomatic in nature: United States policy toward the Open Door in China, and more acutely, the administration's position vis-à-vis the nations of the Caribbean Basin. The former was in truth incidental to Wilson's concern about world order, the latter altogether crucial to his evolving vision of the future in that respect. Regarding commercial relations with China the president was unwilling to endorse a proposal that American banks join a consortium to provide China with investment capital. His reasoning was simple, such a move rendered China dependent on the powers whereas he believed the proper American policy was to protect that country's sovereignty. Some years later Wilson opposed The Twenty-One Demands put forth by the Japanese, which, if implemented, would have reduced China once again to a "geographic expression." Two considerations should be factored into his position: the moral right of China to be politically and economically independent and secondly, just possibly, fear that Japan intended to upset the balance of power in the Far East, which, since the start of the century, had produced stability in that part of the world.[16]

In the Caribbean when dealing with the Central American republics Wilson's understanding of the Monroe Doctrine, that rendering of law and order on a hemispheric scale, found him sounding a strongly moralistic note. It appears, upon contemplation, that as a general proposition "morality and not expediency is the thing that must guide us," as Wilson explained in an address before the Commercial Congress in Mobile, Alabama in 1913. He spoke in favor of reshaping the whole relationship between the Latin American states and the advanced industrial powers. There should be no more concessions to foreign investors: henceforth the United States would encourage investments without concessions on terms set down by the nations themselves. Wilson sought to emphasize his stand by appeal to political morality when he said: "I would rather belong to a poor nation which is free than to a rich nation that had ceased to be in love with liberty."[17] How such lofty Wilsonian ideals were to affect United States relations with individual countries—Venezuela, Costa Rica, the Dominican Republic, Haiti, and Mexico—reveal the mix of morality and politics that characterized the president's foreign policy throughout his time in office.

"Just government rests always upon the consent of the governed" became Wilson's operating principle in United States–Latin American affairs. Being close to the Caribbean Basin nations, and made the more so by American presence at Panama, the president believed he had a special responsibility to promote democratic rule wherever possible. He proposed to make democratic principles "the basis of mutual intercourse, respect, and helpfulness between our sister republics and ourselves. We shall lend our influence of every kind to the realization of these principles in fact and in practice." An explicit commitment indeed. He did not have long to wait to test the validity of his propositions.[18] A 1915 revolution in Haiti brought chaos ushering in a government of men, not a government of laws. Wilson believed he had no choice but to intervene to save lives and property. Troops were landed, occupying the capital, Port-au-Prince and its adjacent countryside. And it was the president's intention American soldiers remain there until "Haitians put men in charge of affairs we can trust to handle affairs and put an end to revolution."[19] Order must prevail, in other words. The very next year similar problems developed in the neighboring state, the Dominican Republic. Once again marines were sent in to restore order, the beginning of a full-fledged occupation that was to last some years. In fact, in the case of the Dominican Republic Wilson went well beyond what Theodore Roosevelt had done. Wilson, it appears, was coming to see that might does not make right, but that might is sometimes needed so that right could prevail.[20]

The Caribbean remained a diplomatic trouble sport. Costa Rica had suffered a military takeover by one Frederico Tinoco who declared himself president. In light of this Wilson refused to recognize the Tinoco regime as legitimate despite pressure from the United Fruit Company and the urging of his former Secretary of State William Jennings Bryan. Wilson's concern for the fitness both of the president of these republics as well as the means of their coming to power was clearly registered in still another instance in 1918. Unfit men should not be allowed to hold office, a proposition he sought to put into effect with respect to President Gomez of Venezuela. After denouncing him as a scoundrel, he inquired of Secretary of State Lansing: "Can you think of any way we can do it that would not upset the peace of Latin America more than letting him alone will?" Again it was a matter of balancing the use of force with the higher objective of keeping the peace.[21]

The ultimate expression of Wilsonian idealism as applied to international affairs in the western hemisphere came in response to an ongoing revolution in Mexico. Unrest there was brewing during the latter stages of the Taft administration and it broke out in full fury in 1913. The president's reflex action to the amorality of Mexican revolutionary politics took effect at once. He was prepared even to the point of sending United States troops south of the Rio Grande because, in his own phrase: "I am going to teach the South American republics to elect good men."[22] His was a strongly willed statement, and a dubious proposition at best as demonstrated by events throughout the region. But perhaps Wilson should not in fact be held to his glibly uttered comment. A more sober judgment was offered when he sent a special message to Congress in April, 1914. It read "the purpose of the United States is solely and singly to secure peace and order in Central America by seeing to it that the processes of self-government were not interrupted or set aside."[23] And surely said processes had suffered a cruel fate with the deposition and murder of President Francisco Madero who had been duly elected to succeed the aging Diaz. The marplot was Victoriana Huerta who proclaimed himself president. Wilson refused to extend recognition to the new regime, his moral sense too deeply offended. As he put it: "the fixed resolve [of United States policy] is that no interruption of civil order will be tolerated. . . . Beyond that fixed purpose the government of the United States will not go."[24] Wilson's moral stance aside, Huerta remained firmly in control. One provocation led to another. An American naval officer and a small contingent of sailors were arrested as they took on supplies at Tampico in the spring of 1914. Wilson ordered the bombardment of Vera Cruz, which resulted in some loss of lives. This resort to force in the name of morality had only negative immediate effects. Huerta was unmoved and his chief political rival, Venustiano Carranza, strongly protested this violation of Mexican sovereignty. The drift toward a second Mexican War was prevented through good offices of Argentina, Brazil, and Chile.

Wilson could not be budged from his stand against Huerta—after all, he was a murderer—despite arguments both in Congress and from the British that if left alone Huerta could restore a reasonable level of law and order. The American president was content to invoke a plan of watchful waiting. It appeared to pay off when Huerta went into voluntary exile, to be succeeded by Carranza, a self-proclaimed reformer. All too soon there occurred a falling out between Carranza and Francisco Villa. Villa has been described as a "picturesque combination of bloodthirsty bandit and Robin Hood."[25] He was in fact a reckless adventurer. He challenged the authority of the duly elected Carranza and "invaded" the United States. On two separate occasions he crossed into American sovereign territory, shooting up towns and killing several dozen American citizens in early 1916. Public opinion was at the boiling point when the President ordered General Pershing at the head of several thousand cavalrymen to cross into Mexico and take Villa dead or alive, a mandate that remained unfulfilled. Yet in this state of affairs Wilson continued to insist that such measures "were employed by the United States to help Mexico save herself and serve her people."[26] His moral purpose never waivered, for better or for worse.

Actions taken by the Wilson administration relative to several Central American states hold considerable promise in explanation of how he arrived at convictions about world order through the device of the League of Nations. That he was not adverse to a limited use of force is obvious. Equally clear, his experience in dealing with these pseudo-republics convinced him that only certain nations were likely to adhere to the "natural law." He was led to conclude that nonrepresentative governments, much less nondemocratic governments, would not be of much use in the task of making the world safe for democracy and less useful in promoting international cooperation. For Wilson and for those he would be working with in 1918–19 it was a Euro-centered world. As of 1916 the president could afford little attention to the minor American nations, so compelling and so worrisome was the war in Europe, and accordingly when might the United States step in and become the arbiter of peace under the guidance of Woodrow Wilson.

It is always wise to guard against reading history backward and Woodrow Wilson's effort to bring about world order is no exception. On the contrary, it is of the utmost importance that care be taken in this regard. Except for the Great War the total of his ideas, hopes, proposals, in short, his contemplations would never had occasion to congeal. A league of nations, much less the League of Nations, could not have marked his career as president or statesman without the war. It is tellingly ironic that death and destruction on an unimaginable scale had to weigh down humanity before world leaders were prepared to move in the direction of establishing a international order under law. When the war broke out no man could have predicted either its course or its outcome: the destruction of empires, the bankruptcy of capitalist nations, the unleashing of revolutionary forces, the millions dead and deformed, body and spirit. Yet given the alliance system and the alacrity with which it swung into action few believed the struggle would be quickly won and victory easy. Sensing all this President Wilson appealed to his countrymen to be neutral in fact and in mind. From the outset he believed the United States as the most powerful neutral nation must stand in support of the rights of all nonbelligerents. To this end he pursued a policy of watchful waiting as he considered what his country could do to bring about an end to the war. That America occupied the moral high ground he was sure, but in light of that what actions could be taken to effect peace without victory?

4

Taft's Realism

WILLIAM HOWARD TAFT ENJOYED A REMARKABLE POST-PRESIDENTIAL career as Yale professor, Co-chairman of the War Industries Board and Chief Justice of the Supreme Court. All the while, down to his appointment to the high court in 1921, he was active in Republican party politics and especially in the peace movement, which eventuated in the proposals for a post World War association or league of nations. In this latter regard and responding to the temper of the era Taft displayed a profound concern for the direction world affairs appeared to be taking, from the Boer War to the Balkan wars. Despite the failure of his treaties of arbitration between the United States and Great Britain and France he remained steadfast in his conviction that unless peaceful means of resolving difficulties among nations were to become available wars of the future would be more fearful and more tragic. Were the mechanisms for arbitration at hand such disasters could be avoided but this could be achieved only if the great nations of the world were led to see the wisdom, and the virtual necessity, of association.

For these reasons Taft welcomed the opportunity to present what he considered an American point of view on the rationale undergirding the international peace movement, which attracted so much attention and support in the wake of The Hague conferences. In 1913 Hamilton Holt, owner and editor of *The Independent*, and himself an advocate of international arbitration, invited Taft to do a series of articles promoting the cause of peace. Taft was quick to respond. His four articles appearing in *The Independent* dealt with the Monroe Doctrine, the protection of the civil rights of resident aliens, treaties of arbitration, and judicial settlement of disputes between sovereign states. An examination of Taft's thinking in each of these matters reveals a mind-set that is positive, optimistic, and decidedly international in outlook.[1]

Regarding the Monroe Doctrine the ex-president denied that force in theory and United States military and naval power in fact had kept the doctrine in tact for upward of a hundred years. Taft argued instead that Washington had maintained the American position by diplomacy and "without firing a single shot."[2] Noting that the United States had been accused of meddling in the internal affairs of nations in the Caribbean and in Central America he stressed that it came down not to efforts to take more territory but to enable those nations to achieve political stability. Stable nations do not invite takeovers by non-American powers. And he went on. "My hope, as an earnest advocate of peace, is that ultimately by international agreement we shall establish a court, like that of The Hague, unto which any government aggrieved by any other government may bring the offending government before an impartial tribunal to answer for its faults and to abide by the judgment of the Court."[3] But such a means of arbitration can not work if governments are not stable and reliable, the very objective of American policy under the Monroe Doctrine. In short, the historical uses of the doctrine have been benign, not selfish. Nonetheless, the fact of American military and naval power, dominant in the western hemisphere, can not be overlooked.

Taft's second area of concern involved the rights of aliens, resident in the United States, the protection of whom was based on treaties. As he stated it "with almost every nation we [the United States] have a treaty in which each contracting party agrees that the nationals of the other party may reside within its jurisdiction, and complying with the laws, may legally pursue their vocation with the same protection to life, liberty and property that the citizens of the contracting country enjoy." And Taft went on to identify this as "perhaps the most common clause" in treaties between sovereign states.[4] Why was he so intent on addressing this issue? The answer comes in two parts. Firstly, the United States had a shameful record of murder, terror, and confiscation of property against foreigners by vigilantes and by mobs. It "is a record in which we can not take pride." Rather we must bow our heads in shame. Secondly, it is a constitutional illusion that the federal government is powerless to address this problem because the police power is a matter of state authority only, whether it is a question of law and order or school segregation. Furthermore, resort to lynching of our own citizens, mostly black males in the southern states, was common enough to desensitize public opinion to such mob action. But Taft was both adamant and persuasive in his counterargument. He insisted that regarding the rights of citizens and aliens "the Federal Government has the power to enact legislation to set down its own administration of justice . . . and has done so."[5] If there is no guarantee of the protection of the two most abused groups, black American citizens and resident aliens, then the protection of all citizens is in some measure jeopardized. Taft is charging that the international obligations imposed by treaties of amity with other nations were not being met. Federal law to remedy this deplorable state of affairs had been proposed a number of times, only to be faced with objections. Taft identified these objections, one by one, and then answered them with convincing counterarguments. He quoted presidents Harrison, McKinley, and Roosevelt, who had addressed the issue and had recommended legislation to Congress as well as quoting directly to the same effect from his own inaugural. Taft focused on the injustices heaped upon the aliens not because he was indifferent to the plight of Afro-Americans but because he was in the process of discussing treaty obligations. He contended that the treaty-making power of the United States was "the widest power it has."[6] "All government power exercised by the country in dealing with foreign governments is exercised by the Federal Government alone, the only limitation upon that power is that in treaties the President and the Senate abide by the constitution. The states have no role in treaty-making."[7] This contention was supported by reference to the decision of the Supreme Court in *Baldwin vs. Frank* (1887). The court asserted that an 1881 treaty between the United States and China that the states of the union were bound by the terms of the treaty, which treaty, of course, provided explicitly that aliens legally residing in the United States enjoyed full rights afforded its own citizens.

Why, it might be asked, did Taft go to such lengths in making his case over a matter that was of little national concern? His purpose was twofold: to arouse the people to a manifest injustice. Between 1885 and 1910 over 150 Chinese aliens and twenty-three Italian immigrants had been murdered. Those figures spoke for themselves. At the same time he was seeking to prevent future incidents he was stressing the necessity of international cooperation on all levels in order to militate against future wars arising, perhaps, from something such as assassination.

Taft's discussion of "arbitration treaties that mean something"— the title of his third article in *The Independent*—began with a lament: the contemporary evidence was convincing "that the dawn of universal peace is not immediately at hand."[8] It became the duty of the United States, in consequence, to promote the cause of peace and order through treaty arrangements, particularly with the nations of the hemisphere. Such a proposition he took for granted so that his attention was turned to the role of Senate in considering general arbitration treaties. "General arbitration" was defined to include "all differences which come within a class of issues as defined in the treaty."[9] The world situation required something more than a mere declaration of a hope that parties to a dispute might conciliate. To be sure Taft recognized that a workable treaty might include reservations but it must also identify specific categories wherein the arbitration must be used. Furthermore, the president, without consulting the Senate, must be the sole judge whether the matter at issue falls within the specifications as stated. In so saying Taft insisted it must be left to the president to judge if the ruling in a particular case involved "national honor" or "vital interests."[10] The Senate should have no hand in the process. Taft compared this executive authority to that of the Interstate Commerce Commission with its discretionary power to judge the fairness of railroad rates.[11] "In the formulation of our treaties it was necessary to hit upon some term which would define a class (of treaty) obligations." Whereupon he quoted from *Hans vs. Louisiana* (1887), a case dealing with a controversy between Kansas and Colorado over water rights, the word "justiciable." By definition "justiciable" meant claims that by their nature were susceptible of decision by the application of the principles of law or equity. The two words taken together should be understood to "comprehend all the rules of international law affecting the rights and duties of nations toward each other."[12] Justiciable, of course, required some kind of tribunal, such as the Court at The Hague or as was stated in the Taft-sponsored arbitration treaties with Great Britain and France, a Joint High Commission.

Much of Taft's argument was drawn from his experience with the above referred to arbitration treaties. His reasoning in rejecting each of the Senate's reservations was presented seriatim, sharply challenging the upper house's action on all points. Taft's closing statement is worth quoting in full.

> The ideal that I would aim at is an arbitral court in which any nation could make complaint against any other nation, and if the complaint is found by the court to be within its jurisdiction, the nation complained against should be summoned, the issue framed by pleadings, and the matter disposed of by judgment. It would, perhaps, sometimes require an international police force to carry out the judgment, but the public opinion of nations would accomplish much. With such a system we could count on a gradual abolishment of armaments and a feeling of the same kind of security that the United States and Canada have to-day which makes armaments and navies on our northern border entirely unnecessary.[13]

In light of Taft's experience as an advocate of law and order he accepted that the rulings of courts or commissions were not self-enforcing and said as much. Hence his reference to an international police force, an adumbration of one of the operating principles of The League to Enforce Peace.

The capstone of "The United States and Peace" came with Taft's discussion of federations considered historically and the promotion of juridical settlements of international disputes. The analysis was at once historical and contemporary in approach. Wishing to demonstrate that "federation" was an instinctive impulse Taft saw it as having a "distinct bearing upon the movement toward international peace."[14] By reviewing, and that in some detail, the history of federation from the Greeks, the Achaian League, through the Holy Roman Empire, the Grand Design of Henry IV, the federation of the Swiss cantons and then on to American history and the creation of the Union of states, Taft argued the inevitability of some form of world organization in the twentieth century, admitting as he did it could take decades, a half a century to come about.[15]

Federation itself was not enough, however. As the constitutional experience of the American union verified a supreme tribunal was an indispensable part of such an organization to adjudicate conflicting claims amongst the member states. Such a tribunal was in keeping with the higher wisdom of the Founding Fathers. The supreme court was given the authority to settle disputes between the once sovereign states, acting as a court of original jurisdiction. For all his infatuation with the American model how could Taft reasonably expect the Hague tribunals to function in meaningful fashion when stakes of a dispute between nations, militarily ready to act, were high? The evidence at hand did not realistically support this turn of events, such was the force of "vital interests" and "national honor" for any of the powers, much less a majority of them. Taft had a profound faith in the majesty of law and a deep-seated conviction judges sitting on international tribunals would be able to rise above loyalty to their nation, as Lord Alverstone had done in the Anglo-American boundary dispute in Alaska earlier in the century. He was looking to the future. Circumstances were far different in 1913 than in 1815 and the Holy Alliance and the concert of Europe. Fresh ideas in political thinking along with a growing fear of a war of multinational dimensions combined to encourage his hopes for the future. Yet Taft betrayed an almost Pollyanna outlook. He asked of himself this question: "How could judgments of such a court be enforced?" to which he gave this response: "I am very little concerned about that. After we have gathered the cases into court and decided, and the judgments embodied in solemn declaration of a court thus established, few nations will care to face the condemnation of international public opinion and disobey the judgment." And should the court be defied "it will be time enough to devise methods to prevent recurrences."[16] To be sure, Taft could have hardly predicted the self-immolation of nations as occurred in World War I and revolutions of nihilism that followed. Nor could he have imagined the United States turning its back on the processes seeking to keep peace through collective security. Taft was preaching a new gospel of internationalism on the eve of the Great War. In this respect note must be made of his willingness to intimate at least that armed force might have to be used to bring about meaningful arbitration. But he appeared to retreat from that position invoking the power of international public opinion . . . a weak reed indeed. Perhaps no more needs to be added than to admit that Taft's realism was not perfectly consistent any more than Woodrow Wilson's idealism was without ambiguity.

Looked at from the perspective of peace and war the year 1914 was oddly paradoxical. The guns of August sounded against thoughts and indeed efforts to achieve a peaceful world associated with The Hague conferences of 1899 and 1907. Plans were afoot for a third such conference some months before August of that year. Peace-minded leaders in the United States, including Andrew White and Joseph Choate, had brought together a citizens' group for the purpose of urging President Wilson to call for such a meeting, only to be told the administration had already taken steps in that direction. Furthermore there were ongoing efforts in Europe proposing possible continental federation. How any of these ideas were to be translated into reality was unclear but the sentiment, if not the conviction, that it must be attempted was in the forefront of the peace movement. The irony of 1914 is complete when it is realized that it would take a war of huge proportions to transform feelings into commitments, whether the device would be Wilson's League of Nations or a League To Enforce Peace as advocated by Taft.

Taft's *The United States and Peace* commentary was part of the flurry of activity with Hamilton Holt one of the leaders aiming to make peace, not war. Using *The Independent* as his forum Holt himself advanced principles upon which some kind of "league of peace" might be founded. Many others, including Irving Fisher, a Yale professor who had gone public with ideas about a "union of nations" and Alton P. Parker, the Democratic presidential candidate in 1904, spoke respectively for academics and Democrats for peace. Indeed some of the best minds and the "best people" were coming aboard the bandwagon. Holt was both the glue and prod in the early stage of the movement. In January, 1915 a conference at the Century Club in New York began the arduous and uncertain task of transforming a host of suggestions into concrete form and within weeks had hammered a set of five essentials, one of which stated that the formation of a league ought to be under the leadership of the United States before the war in Europe was over.

The essence of Taft's realism regarding peace among nations was contained in an official statement issued by the League To Enforce Peace, as the movement was identified. It came into being 17 June 1915 at a historic meeting in Independence Hall, Philadelphia. Some three hundred people, mostly notables, were in attendance. A statement setting forth the purpose and means to that purpose, given the solemn title, Warrant From History, became the platform of the new league. It read as follows.

Warrant from History

Throughout five thousand years of recorded history peace, here and there established, has been kept, and its area has been widened, in one way only. Individuals have combined their efforts to suppress violence in the local community. Communities have co-operated to maintain the authoritative state and to preserve peace within its borders. States have formed leagues or confederations, or have otherwise co-operated, to establish peace among themselves. Always peace has been made and kept, when made and kept at all, by the superior power of superior numbers acting in unity for the common good.

Mindful of this teaching of experience, we believe and solemnly urge that the time has come to devise and to create a working union of sovereign nations to establish peace among themselves and to guarantee it by all known and available sanctions at their command, to the end that civilization may be conserved, and the progress of mankind in comfort, enlightenment and happiness may continue.

It is desirable for the United States to join a league of nations binding the signatories to the following:

First: All justiciable questions arising between the signatory powers, not settled by negotiation shall, subject to the limitations of treaties, be submitted to a judicial tribunal for hearing and judgment, both upon the merits and upon any issue as to its jurisdiction of the question.

Second: All other questions arising between the signatories and not settled by negotiation, shall be submitted to a Council of Conciliation for hearing, consideration and recommendation.

Third: The signatory powers shall jointly use forthwith both their economic and military forces against any one of their number that goes to war, or commits acts of hostility against another of the signatories before any question arising shall be submitted as provided in the foregoing.

Fourth: Conferences between the signatory powers shall be held from time to time to formulate and codify rules of international law, which, unless some signatory shall signify its dissent within a stated period, shall thereafter govern in the decisions of the Judicial Tribunal mentioned in Article One.[17]

These principles had emerged from long and frequent discussions by like-minded proponents. Within two weeks of the Philadelphia meeting a permanent organization for the League was established. William Howard Taft was named president and A. Lawrence Lowell chairman of the executive committee. Immediately newspapers and magazines gave League activities full coverage and a pamphlet series was launched all aimed at getting the purpose and the promise of the undertaking more widely known. For example, in an article appearing in *Atlantic Monthly* for September, 1915 (and summarized in *Literary Digest* that same month) Dr. Lowell, president of Harvard, wrote with moderation about the League's purpose—it was not designed to end World War I but rather to prevent the possibility of World War II—in order to gain recognition and support.[18] What the League's Warrant had done was to take the basic proposition of Taft's 1912 proposed treaties with London and Paris to a crucial next step by calling for a resort to force, economic and/or military, to halt aggression. It would be "a giant leap for mankind" should it be agreed to by the Powers at the war's end.

So widespread had been the sentiment for peace in the years leading up to 1914 that no less a man of martial instincts than Theodore Roosevelt could be moved to speak out in favor of some sort of peace league. The occasion of his widely reported remarks was a 1910 visit to Christiania, Norway in connection with the Nobel Peace Prize, which he had won in 1906. In his remarks in Norway he offered two pregnant observations. First, it would be a "master stroke" were the leading nations to form a league of peace, and in addition he stressed the need to organize an international brigade to police the peace processes. These were heady thoughts, which can be understood largely as an expression of the "spirit of the occasion."[19] The very next year found Roosevelt attacking Taft's treaties of arbitration as both foolish and dangerous to America's national honor and vital interests. But even if the warlike Teddy succumbed but briefly to the peace fever, he nonetheless had responded positively to "the spirit of the times" and in so doing may have encouraged others to think in terms of peace, not war. As for Taft, whose falling out with Roosevelt was virtually complete by 1912, he took heart from the seeming support of Elihu Root, himself a winner of the Nobel Prize for Peace in 1912, and Senator Lodge who in years down to 1917 spoke approvingly of Taft's position on world order in the postwar era. More important still was the evident acceptance by President Wilson who all but endorsed a league of nations along the lines laid down by the Taft-Lowell-Holt way of thinking.

A more careful assessment of the Root-Lodge-Wilson attitudes toward the league suggests that Taft, either out of a need to feel these important leaders were with him or due to a belief once the war was over both Republicans and Democrats alike would favor Taft's version of an ordered world, reveals his miscalculation. Yet Taft was not altogether blameworthy inasmuch as at the end of 1916 Wilson's plan was not on the table and as of that date Root, Lodge, and Wilson were at the least on the fence. True enough, Root never affiliated himself with the league largely because he rejected the proposal the United States be conjoined with other nations in enforcing the will of the league, although it has been said "his mind was constantly moving in that direction."[20] No doubt Root's association with the league would have lent it greater credence and both Taft and Lowell pleaded with him to join them but he could not oblige them because of what he considered would lead to diplomatic entanglement.

If Root acted on principle Lodge was guided by political considerations in his attitude toward Taft and the league. Never having joined formally, he was nonetheless attracted to it on two counts. He announced his willingness to stand behind proposals calling for the use of force to maintain collective security. In June, 1915 in a commencement address at Union College he stated his position accordingly. "The peace of the world can only be maintained . . . as the peace of a single nation is maintained by force which united nations are willing to put behind the peace and order in the world." The league also appealed to Lodge because it was overwhelmingly republican in origin and leadership and thus could be used to spike the guns of the Brynites who were against any show of military power, even of military preparedness. It is small wonder Taft believed his fellow Republican would grow in the direction of advocating the "concepts" of the league when in May, 1916 he joined President Wilson as a guest speaker at a conclave of the league supporters in the nation's capital. Lodge reiterated the assertions he had made at Union College referring to the postwar period as a "Utopia" of "united nations." The thrust and flavor of what he said is conveyed in the following excerpts. "The limit of voluntary arbitration, I think, has been reached. . . . The next step is that which the League proposes and that is to put force behind international peace, an international league or agreement or tribunal, for peace. We may not solve it that way, but if we cannot solve it in that way, it can be solved in no other. . . . The way the problem must be worked out must be left to this League and to those who are giving this great question the study it deserves. I know how quickly we shall be met with the statement that this is a dangerous question . . . that no nation can submit to the judgment of other nations . . . I know the difficulties that arise when we speak of anything which seems to involve an alliance. But I do not believe when Washington warned us against entangling alliances he meant for one moment we should not join with other civilized nations of the world if a method could be found to avoid war and encourage peace."[21] What then, given such an outcry, prevented Lodge from joining actively in promoting the work of the league? He appears to have stood at an ideological crossroad. Unhappy with a Democrat as president, his personal antipathy toward Wilson was egged on by Theodore Roosevelt's openly expressed contempt for the administration's policy of neutrality. Lodge, it can be said, was of two minds, which Taft was unlikely to grasp; quite simply he took the Senator at his public word. But in private correspondence Lodge expressed himself as "fighting shy" of the league—that was in October. At the end of 1916 he wrote James Bryce, one of the prominent British advocates of some kind of peace association, in this vein. "What can be done with a league of peace in the future, I do not know. We must try our best . . . but the obstacles are enormous."[22]

When the United States entered the war just a few months later and Wilson was not only commander-in-chief but the statesman to whom fell the responsibility of shaping America's place in the new world order Lodge became one of the leaders of the opposition. At the same time the viability of the League To Enforce Peace became problematic. But before all this took place it is necessary to examine Wilson's attitude toward the league from 1915 to 1917.

President Wilson's acceptance of ex-President Taft's invitation to address the League To Enforce Peace gathering made for a notable event in itself. Three of the leading public men of the day coming together to sustain a common cause, notable the more so because it gave the peace movement a bipartisan character that was newsworthy indeed. Furthermore, Wilson took the opportunity presented him to stress his endorsement of a postwar league of the world's nations. With Wilson, Lodge, and Taft occupying a common ground America's active part in an organization dedicated to peace seemed assured. At first the president had kept his distance from the league. He was put off in part by the fact it was Republican dominated. And Wilson being Wilson wanted to be sure that his own understanding of what the American position should be, as the outcome of the war became more certain, was not to be compromised by association with the league. In any case he decided to go public in preparing his remarks. He stressed the time had come when the United States must recognize that it had to be an active partner in the global family. "The interests of all nations are our own also." Referring to the outbreak of the war he insisted that system of secret treaties made the struggle inevitable, in part at least because there was no agency to mediate the conflicting demands between the two sides. Such a situation must not be allowed to prevail in the future. Whereupon the president moved to the centerpiece of his statement in which he approved and espoused the long range purpose of the league, namely, to achieve world order through a world organization brought into existence for that very purpose. Wilson was breaking new ground in his own name and that of the nation.

> This is undoubtedly the thought of America. This is what we ourselves will say when there comes proper occasion to say it. In the dealings of nations with one another, arbitrary force must be rejected and we must move forward to the thought of the modern world, the thought of which peace is the very atmosphere. That thought constitutes a chief part of the passionate conviction of America.
>
> We believe these fundamental things: First, that every people has a right to choose the sovereignty under which they shall live. . . . Second, that the small states of the world have a right to enjoy the same respect for their sovereignty and for their territorial integrity that great and powerful nations expect and insist upon. And, third, that the world has a right to be free from every disturbance of its peace that has its origin in aggression and disregard of the rights of peoples and nations. So sincerely do we believe in these things that I am sure that I speak the mind and wish of the people of America when I say that the United States is willing to become a partner in any feasible association of nations formed in order to realize these objects and make them secure against violation.
>
> If it should ever be our privilege to suggest or initiate a movement for peace among the nations now at war, I am sure that the people of the United States would wish their government to move along these lines. First, such a settlement with regard to their own immediate interests as the belligerents may agree upon. We have nothing material of any kind to ask for ourselves, and are quite aware that we are in no sense or degree parties to the present quarrel. Our interest is only in peace and its future guarantees. Second, an universal association of

the nations to maintain the inviolate security of the highway of the seas for the common and unhindered use of all the nations of the world, and to prevent any war begun either contrary to treaty covenants or without warning and full submission of the causes to the opinion of the world—a virtual guarantee of territorial integrity and political independence.[23]

This lengthy passage is a telling one. Wilson had not only seconded the purpose of the league, he was also careful to include as its objectives a guarantee of territorial integrity and the self-determination of peoples in matters of their form of government. These principles would become prominent features of the president's outlook, bearing fruit in the covenant of the League of Nations. As president of the League To Enforce Peace, Taft must have taken heart from hearing the president of the United States weigh in so heavily on the concept and purpose of a league.

Taft himself made any number of speeches in various parts of the country and to different interest groups, proselytizing in the name of the League To Enforce Peace. There was a good bit of carryover from one address to another, yet in almost every instance he was able to single out important particulars for closer consideration. It is almost as though in the process of preparing his remarks he gained new insights and fresh arguments to undergird his advocacy of the league. By nature Taft was a diligent scholar, which stands out as he discussed in-depth the history of nations associating for a common purpose. For example, in an address before the World Court Congress at Cleveland in May, 1915, even as the league was forming, Taft went to great lengths to represent the proposed world organization as a natural descendant of Anglo-Saxon and therefore Anglo-American governmental development. He presented a learned but not argumentative account drawn from the historical record. He faced up to the principle that force must be utilized as an ultimate sanction on one nation's behavior toward another. He was careful to explain to the first annual assemblage of the League that such a warrant "only furnishes the instrumentality of force to prevent attack . . . It is believed that is more practical than to attempt to enforce judgment after a hearing." Force would be used only to challenge "palpable violation of the obligation of members." As he was to reiterate it was wise not to be overly ambitious at the start: better to allow for an evolution of methods of order over time.[24]

One of the more persistent criticisms of United States involvement in the league or any league for that matter was the Warrant violated the Constitution. Taft, the consummate authority of such issues as might arise with the league in being, met the questions head-on, rendering them null and void. The contention was submission of a dispute to which the United States was a party to an international tribunal for a hearing amounted to an abandonment of the treaty-making shared by the president and the senate. Here is Taft's rejoinder: "The United States is a nation, and from the foreign stand point, a sovereign nation, without limitation of its sovereignty. It may therefore, through its treaty making power consent to any agreement with other powers relating to a subject matter that is usually considered and made the subject of treaties." To solidify his position in the matter he cited the opinion of the Supreme Court in *Geoffrey vs. Riggs* 113 U.S. 258. "The treaty power of the United States as expressed in the Constitution is unlimited, except by those restraints which are found in that instrument against the actions of the Government." The reasoning behind such an interpretation resonates the ruling of John Marshall in *McCullough vs. Maryland* and with Taft's admiration for the jurisprudence of the first great chief justice he was all the more comfortable. To put the matter directly: the treaty-making power allows any agreement not expressly forbidden by the Constitution.

The second recurring doubt about constitutionality was the exercise of military force, which opponents contended undercut the power of the Congress, and the Congress alone, to declare war. To disarm this contention Taft adroitly drew on the 1904 treaty in which the United States guaranteed the political independence and territorial integrity of the Republic of Panama. In practice what this guarantee meant came to this: if Panama were invaded or its sovereignty was in any way compromised the United States, under the treaty, would act immediately to fend off the invader. No declaration of war by Congress would be required. But there would be no thought that the Congress had in consequence surrendered its war making power or had had it usurped.[25]

Taking advantage of what he surmised would be a friendly reception by the National Education Association members meeting in New York City in July, 1916, Taft described the league as "a constructive plan for human betterment." Although he took his listeners over familiar ground he struck out in a new direction, insisting that civilization itself might well hang in the balance, so dangerous was a future world lacking in a structure designed to provide international order under law. Just as in domestic affairs restraints were necessary to curb the unruly, so also in world affairs. Only the "theoretical anarchist" envisioned life without a workable social compact. Taft was making his appeal in the name of mankind. At the close of his remarks he advised the educators present that both President Wilson and Senator Lodge had "approved the principles" of the League To Enforce Peace, adding the names of Sir Edward Grey, British Foreign Secretary and Lord Bryce, each widely known and respected in the United States as lending "sympathy and support" along with that of Aristide Briand, French Minister of Foreign Affairs.[26]

It is appropriate to turn to one additional Taft plea for the league, before the president, in January, 1918, announced his idea for the League of Nations. At a Chamber of Commerce dinner in Queens, New York City, he introduced a new tactic. Instead of going over still again the basics of the league, by this date well understood, Taft singled out three leading opponents of The League, aiming his shafts directly at each. He seemed to take personal satisfaction, and understandably so, when he accused Theodore Roosevelt of failing to read and comprehend what was proposed about the use of force. Roosevelt implied that every compromise reached by the league tribunal would be put into effect forcibly if necessary. This was such a drastic misreading of the document "We can therefore dismiss further consideration of Mr. Roosevelt's objection." Senator William Borah's opposition Taft found based on several sets of contrived possibilities, for example, Japan acquiring Mexican territory by treaty and therefore a violation of the Monroe Doctrine, which seemed so improbable as not to take seriously. Again a wave of the hand in dismissal. William Jennings Bryan's pacifism was treated more kindly, Taft gently reminding his rival that the Bryan treaties of arbitration of 1913 were consistent with the rationale of the league.[27]

Taken all in all the president of the League To Enforce Peace had done a creditable job of explanation cum defense of the practical approach to world order, which he hoped would become a postwar reality. He appeared to relish his part in the campaign to sell enforcement as the critical, and distinctive element, as various statesmen struggled to lead civilized nations away from the abyss of still another great war.

In late 1916 Solon Fieldman, president of Press Forum Inc. of New York invited William Howard Taft and William Jennings Bryan, one of the leading critics of the League To Enforce Peace, to a published debate regarding its merits. Taft replied almost at once, saying "that a joint discussion in the public press will help make clear to the American People and the World what is necessary in the way of fraternal cooperation of Nations to avoid and suppress war." Bryan was equally agreeable to Fieldman's proposal. "I shall be pleased to participate in the debate in the hope that a careful consideration of the arguments for and against these specific and concrete proposals may aid in establishing that which is best to our country and the world." In subsequent correspondence with Fieldman Taft explained: "The League will involve this nation in serious obligations. If those obligations are not met promptly and willingly, it is far better that we should not enter the League at all. The best means of avoiding failure to meet the obligations of the League by the United States is to have the people advised in advance exactly what the League is, what burden it will entail, and what sacrifices will have to be made in order to accomplish its purposes, so that when the President and the Senate shall sign the treaty, they will be doing an act, the full purport of which and the future consequences of which the people will understand, approve and be willing to meet." Writing in such a vein it becomes plain that Taft had great faith in the instrument, and enough determination to go forward with it.[28]

The format of the debate affords ample opportunity to examine, compare, and evaluate the realism of Taft's approach to the peacemaking and peace-keeping processes. It was agreed there would be three separate but closely related questions: (1) Was the platform of the league feasible? (2) Did the platform furnish the most practical plan for securing permanent peace once the war was over? (3) Should the United States become a signatory to a treaty designed to enforce peace? The analysis that follows concentrates on the elements of Taft's arguments demonstrating the realism of his position: it is less concerned with Bryan except when what he argued helps to draw Taft out in counterpoint. For the purpose here it is not a case of winning the debate or losing it. And it is also well to bear in mind that neither Taft nor Bryan was officially empowered and therefore less restricted in their arguments.

Taft began his effort noting the platform of the League only laid down a broad outline of a plan. But to begin with, courts of international justice were not a totally new concept: and experience had shown they could function effectively. Certainly there would arise irritating and threatening issues that may not be settled on principles of law so that compromise would be the next, practical step. As for the force factor Taft insisted it gave "vitality" to the proposal. "It appeals to practical men." So it was in domestic politics and so it must be in international politics. As for the conferences or congresses called for, again, past experience at the Hague meetings had spelled out the potential for positive outcomes. The league, as proposed, was to be a "world alliance" replacing the competing alliances, which had helped to bring on war in 1914.[29]

Following upon that contention in his second argument Taft insisted the League was not a defensive alliance against outside nations. "Its purpose is to furnish a means of keeping peace among its members only." Within the league the use of force would be a last resort. Diplomatic pressure, negotiations, and appeals to common interests would naturally precede the call for economic, or military force. Economic pressure could be a powerful deterrent and probably make military action unnecessary. Furthermore, the fear of forcible restraint is "often an indispensable motive to strengthen the moral impulse to obey the right." Fear and force have their place in the affairs of nations not less than in the lives of the people. Sounding a contemporary note Taft exclaimed: "What was it but force that freed Cuba from oppression?" Bryan, of course, was reluctant to endorse the use of force, especially armed force, and he asked for definition or example of what would constitute economic pressure. Taft responded indicating boycotting as the likely weapon. Embargo, threatened or imposed, by all members of the league against the troublesome nation he deemed proper. And he reminded Bryan and his supporters that all action taken, of whatever nature, would be confined to the league. In the spirit of give-and-take Bryan shot back in a fashion suggesting red herrings or plain baiting. For example, he accused Taft (and his league) of "still worshiping the scimitar." Nothing else will do. He also added the arms manufacturers (the merchants of death) would be delighted to continue to profit at the expense of the league members.

Wanting to emphasize the practical character of league operations Taft was at pains to underscore the limits of its actions. It would seek to impose the judgments of the tribunal provided for in the League mandate. It was quite another matter to enforce the outcome of a compromise unless it involved a principle of law. For the most part Taft viewed the terms of a compromise moral and not legal obligations. In so many words: "It is wise for us not to try too much, lest being over ambitious, it fail." This was not to weaken his contention that force was a needed ingredient in the overall scheme of things but that its exercise had to be carefully defined and prudently applied. For our league, he reiterated, the force factor was vital. This assertion Bryan dismissed by terming the force plank in the League platform a "sort of gattling-gun attachment." The former secretary of state preferred to substitute "promote" for "force" in naming the League. His plan for a series of arbitration agreements lacked any coordination agency to appeal to. Taft objected, saying it was not a step in the direction of a world political organization.[30]

At this juncture in the exchange assertions by both men were arguments largely reiterative, preliminary to heart of the matter: should the United States become a signatory to the league platform? Taft advanced two reasons why the nation should join in the peace plan, and Bryan replied with three objections. The ex-president recognized the position of the United States as unique. It was the most populous of the developed nations, save Russia, which was in a state of chaos, and had both a material and a moral duty to act to prevent future wars. As for the employment of American armed forces they would be fighting as part of an international military operation. Although it was not mentioned the combined units of various countries had acted together to rescue hostages and raise the siege of Peking at the time of the Boxer Rebellion—a case in point. Bryan's rejoinder was equally direct. The whole proposal went against Washington's dictum regarding entangling alliances: American vital interests were not European in nature: the Monroe Doctrine would be sacrificed. Taft countered on all points. The League was not an alliance: national interests were worldwide in fact; the Monroe Doctrine had always rested ultimately on force, should any one had chosen to challenge it.[31]

Toward the close of the debate Bryan brought up President Wilson's message to Congress of January, 1917 in which he advanced his own propositions for attaining a just and lasting peace. Taft replied that in May, 1916, when at a dinner sponsored by the League To Enforce Peace the president spoke approvingly of the League and what it stood for. This spirited exchange of viewpoints had undoubtedly served the purpose its sponsor had in mind. By the time the last words were spoken the United States had gone to war, which to Bryan was a frightening fact. Certain as he was of the outcome now the United States was in the fight, Taft looked forward to an Allied victory and thus the opportunity to mend a tattered world through the application of a practical and workable machinery as a guarantee of the future peace of the world.[32]

Until such time as Woodrow Wilson, with all the advantage of being president of the United States, came forth with his League of Nations plan William Howard Taft was the most prominent advocate in American public life of a postwar world organization. By speaking and writing in explanation and support of the League To Enforce Peace as he did, Taft personified the elder statesman who came to the task of outlining the way to order with clean hands. If he was a Republican by party affiliation he was first of all an American. While the total of his views on international affairs did not coincide with those of President Wilson nonetheless he put his faith in the principle rather than in the particulars of a league. At the end of the day, in the wake of the turmoil of the fight over Wilson's League of Nations, and its rejection by the Senate Taft could still proclaim that, if he had been a senator at the time he would have voted for Wilson's League, with reservations or without reservations. Such was his commitment to the cause of peace.

5
Wilson's Higher Realism

Woodrow Wilson's name is inextricably linked to the League of Nations. As seen by contemporaries his was the animating force behind the league and historians have authenticated this view. The instrument setting up a league or association of nations was a logical progression from the Fourteen Points. But bonding Wilson and the league as though he had sired it was something that happened in the course of that short period of time between the autumn of 1918 and the spring of 1921. The hope for a workable association of nations was, of course, a commonplace from the onset of the twentieth century and continuing during the war years. In late 1917 the Balfour government in London authorized Sir Walter Phillimore to work out some notions in this regard and in the war cabinet Lord Robert Cecil and Jan Christian Smuts gave the proposition strong support. Another British voice in support of a league was that of Lord Bryce, well known in the United States. On the American side the League To Enforce Peace had put forth proposals that appealed to a great many influential people, Woodrow Wilson among them. Colonel House had thought about and studied approaches to the problem of postwar arrangements and from him the president had garnered a number of ideas. On a less formal level he had discussed the matter in some detail with his brother-in-law, Dr. Stockton Axson. As he had joined the American Peace Society and was growing more and more cognizant of the ever expanding attention given to the international brotherhood of the workers of the world Wilson found himself persuaded that only cooperation between governments could meet the challenge. The president's promotion of the idea of Pan-Americanism, contained in an address to the Pan-American Science Congress in January of 1916, bears this out. He talked about "the foundations of amity in a world of peace and order" for the Americas. Personal convictions, encouragement from friends and advisors, aware of the widespread desire of men of learning and mill and factory workers for peace, all this and more fed Wilson's determination to endorse a league of nations, which for him became the League of Nations.

In so saying three considerations must be kept in mind, perhaps the most important of which is that Wilson, unlike Taft and his associates, bore the full burden of responsibility for American foreign policy as president. This was bound to shape his outlook. When this is linked to a passionate morality and an extreme sense of personal privacy, even in dealing with affairs of state, which can be interpreted as supreme egotism, it becomes understandable why Wilson was resolved to have the league reflect his private vision.

Certain characteristics of Wilson's public philosophy became essentials of the covenant he displayed in a 4 July 1914 address on practical politics. Democracy as the best if not the only political way of life was strongly urged. In part he said: "If I did not believe that the moral judgment would be the last judgment . . . I could not believe in popular government. . . . I earnestly believe in the democracy not only of America but of every awakened people that wishes and intends to gain control over its own affairs." This statement may well mark an important juncture in Wilson's public expression of long held beliefs, anticipating the axiom of "making the world safe for democracy." In closing this address he emphasized "those moral inspirations which lie at the basis of all freedom," that America "has lifted high the light which will . . . guide the feet of mankind to justice, liberty and peace." Such were Wilson's convictions as well as his sentiments on the eve of the Great War.[1]

The president's response to the outbreak of hostilities was that of strict neutrality—neutral in thought, word and deed—as the one way the moral force of the United States could be exercised during, or if it came to that, after the war. But how to translate Wilson's public morality into law, into international law, thereby achieving an ordered world? During the early days of the war the president confided his peace formula to Stockton Axson. Axson recalled how the conversation revealed an organized if somewhat general series of principles. Four in number, the first was that all nations, small and large alike, must have equal right to sovereignty. This was closely linked to the proposition that "never again" should territory be exchanged as a result of conquest. In order to reduce the prospect of future wars governments and not private firms—the so-called merchants of death—must own the arms manufacturing industries. Finally, there must come about some greater association of all nations whereby each nation shall be guaranteed integrity to which proposition "any one nation violating the agreement between all of them shall bring punishment on itself automatically." According to *The New York Times* Axson was uncertain if the term "association" or "league" was used but given the full statement it makes little difference regarding Wilson's position.[2]

The president's relationship with Axson was personal and therefore the more likely to be unguarded. Although Colonel House may well have been Wilson's confidante, without portfolio, he remained a subordinate who had less influence at times than he wanted to believe. But at least at one major juncture in their exchange over league formulae, the Magnolia conference, 15 August 1918, it appeared both men were on the same page, responding to each other *ex aequo.* Wilson's obduracy regarding his personal privacy nonetheless drew a line that neither House nor others were allowed to cross. Quite simply this was an implacable part of his makeup. Wilson relied on House for information and opinion, but the question remains was his advice consistently influential. The colonel was enlightened and persistent in efforts to allay war and promote peace before the conflict broke out.[3] In May, 1914, he was abroad talking in London and Berlin about an Anglo-German naval detente. Within the month in conversation with Sir Cecil Spring Rice and Sir William Tyrrell he again discussed plans "for international cooperation with a constructive purpose." According to Charles Seymour "it was the same plan he had discussed with (Walter Hines) Page and (Count) Bernstorff, a plan to bring the Great Powers of the world into a general undertaking for the development and protection of the backward regions of the world, and it contained the germ of the mandatory scheme later worked out in the League of Nations."[4] This plan House, with the approval of both Spring Rice and Tyrrell, presented to Sir Edward Grey. Again it should be noted he confided all this fully to the president. He also took the occasion to share his thoughts with David Lloyd George.

House continued to think peace even as the war raged on. He urged the two main belligerents, Germany and Great Britain, to compromise their war aims, and sought to involve Wilson in his scheme. In so acting the Colonel badly misread Wilson's determination to remain neutral rather than throw the support of the United States against the nation that would not agree to a planned settlement. Reading history backwards we know House was chasing a ghost that could not be caught. But as utterly committed as he was to his peculiar plan for peace, in reality a kind of peace without victory, his ongoing interaction with the president might have played out otherwise. At the very least, Colonel House was in phase with Wilson's own private yearning for peace. Wilson's amour propre was not the only impediment facing Colonel House. The second Mrs. Wilson née Edith Bolling, married the president in December, 1915 and took an almost instant dislike to the colonel. This personal discord had its likeliest source in the First Lady's determination to brook no competition in matters of advice given her husband. As later events would show she was a woman of imperious will and Colonel House was the first of the Wilson coterie to feel her influence because of his long and close association with the president.[5]

To stress the point again, unlike Taft, President Wilson presided over the foreign policy of the most powerful neutral nation in the world. The United States had historic and everyday connections with Great Britain, France, and Germany. The "special relationship" with Britain dated from 1898 and had grown stronger with the passing years. What patriotic American could forget the aid France extended during the War for Independence, of which the Marquis de Lafayette was both symbol and presence? On the other hand, as even the British ambassador Spring Rice warned his government, there were twelve million German-Americans composing the largest single foreign born element in the nation.[6] Their sentiment for the fatherland could not be ignored. Nonetheless Wilson was to keep the vital interests of the United States, his ultimate responsibility relative to the European war, foremost in this thinking, planning, and policies. All this put certain restraints on the president. He could not allow himself to give way to his feelings, and he could ill afford to take the nation in one direction and then do a turnabout because of new developments on land or sea. Yet his conduct of diplomacy he might want to reconsider. Violation of Belgian neutrality in 1914, for example, contributed to Wilson's moral outrage and his political compulsion to look to protect small nations from such attacks in the future. Very likely the sinking of the *Lusitania* in May, 1915, put his temper to the supreme test. Over one thousand passengers, including one hundred Americans, died when the ship was torpedoed by a German submarine. Yet Wilson sensed, understood, perhaps even divined, that it was not the time to draw the sword, however great his sense of moral outrage.

Morality had long dominated his outlook. Wilson was sincere in his contention, for example, that progressive democracy and Christianity could be properly identified one in the other. The war against human greed and exploitation of the weak might be won, and indeed was being one, he told a large audience of the Protestant faithful in 1911. Inevitably he transposed his moral precepts to war and peace. Wilson's religious avowals were consistent with the introspective side of his character. He dwelt often on the kind of person he was. This same introspection fed Wilson's self-reliance. His practice of appealing over the heads of state and national legislatures—and one day over that of the United States Senate—for vindication by the people was one way his self-confidence manifested itself. Self-esteem was part of his hubris, which was to become his nemesis.

Woodrow Wilson's moral purpose was so deeply rooted it could on occasion invite ridicule, if not contempt. One of the scathing terms of denunciation directed at him when he was president was "Presbyterian priest." A curious insult but one that was more than an alliterative catch phrase. An enduring commitment to the theological tenets of covenant Presbyterianism guided him in his public life. But why "priest"? In religious invective "priest" is often used as a word of scorn, one that easily shades into such terms as "priestcraft" or "priest ridden." It was the absolute certainty of the rectitude of his policies, his vision, and his League of Nations, what opponents derided as his moral arrogance that has been called his glory and his shame. As "Presbyterian" told of his status as one of the elect of God, one of his "saints," so "priest" reinforced the impression of one who always thought of himself as doing God's work here on earth. All this suggests, in a perverse way, how vital were religious beliefs in President Wilson's conduct of affairs. Yet the world in which he lived remained unconverted, like the saints of the primitive church Wilson dwelt *in partibus infidelium*. Undaunted, at critical junctures he could be all the more determined to make people and situations conform to his purpose and his will. Elected by God for His service he consistently judged himself as doing God's work. At the most crucial time in his public life, the fight over the league, this compulsion was to impart to him a messiah complex, and a puzzle to those at home and abroad who had to deal with him. It was his consistently morally guided diplomacy, in 1914-18, which had conditioned him to believe that he could part the waters of injustice and avoid a victors' peace. As a review and analysis of his morality based diplomacy shows, Woodrow Wilson came to believe in himself as the one man who possessed the office, the will, and the right to reorder the world.

By definition wars offend moral sensitivities. The greater the military action the more occasions to try men's souls. Loss of life, maiming of bodies, property destruction, and dislocation of people when combined in such a conflict as raged for four years in Europe and environs constituted an assault on morality. So much was this the case that it brought to a close a period of world history in process for four hundred years. Nationalism as a movement among and between states had run on its own sword. Reared in the shadow of one of the most ferocious internecine struggles of the epoch Woodrow Wilson had absorbed, partly by osmosis, and by study and reflection, the lesson that modern war brought the dark side of human nature to the fore. Certain of his feelings as found in his First Inaugural, he spoke of a public morality that would be severely tested in the fires of the Great War, which in March, 1913, was a gathering storm. "This is the high enterprise of the new day: to lift everything that concerns our life as a Nation to the light that shines from the hearthfire of every man's conscience and vision of the right. This is not a day of triumph, this is a day of dedication . . . I summon all honest men, all patriotic, all forward looking men to my side. God helping me I will not fail them, if they but will counsel and sustain me."[7] Although Wilson would have had in mind domestic issues and reforms rather than world order the sense of moral purpose permeating his message had a universal application. Within a week of taking office the new president advised members of the diplomatic corps that "just government rests always on the consent of the governed and . . . there can be no freedom without order based upon law and upon the public conscience and approval. We shall look to make these principles the basis of mutual intercourse, respect and helpfulness . . . We shall lend our influence of every kind to the realization of these principles in fact and practice."[8] Unknowingly but fatefully Wilson was girding his loins for dealing with a mind bending challenge to human dignity: the trench warfare, the poison gas, the barbed wire, the hours long bombardments, the shell shock, the disappearance of a generation. As events would demonstrate Wilson was not a peace at any price man, but neither could he be indifferent to the wholesale suffering the war, when it came in full fury, was to inflict. The amorality of the moment was spelled out by the German Chancellor, Bethemann-Hollweg, who dismissed his country's treaty to respect Belgian neutrality as: "just a scrap of paper" thereby setting the moral tone of the war itself. From the beginning Wilson underwent a conditioning that step by step, convinced him of the urgency of moral regeneration through a device like an association or a league of nations. The more distended the war became, the more determined he was to broker a lasting peace.

This conditioning process is exemplified in his official response to the sacrifice of Belgian neutrality to imperial German war aims and Wilson's reaction to the sinking of the *Lusitania* nine months later. The president took no public position on the fate of Belgium despite the bombing of Antwerp, an undefended city, in a dirigible attack and the mass of evidence of German perfidy presented to the United States government by a Belgian delegation. It may be objected that the loss of American lives on the ill-fated *Lusitania* struck much closer to home than the invasion of a small European country—all of which underscores the workings of conditioning as a factor in Wilson's outlook on the war. As the conflict wore on the disasters mounted with skies over the war zone growing darker and darker. Wilson was made to see that an appeal to the high realism—statesmanship infused by moral precepts—pointed to the only way out of the morass. It becomes appropriate here to lay out more specifically what is to be understood as Woodrow Wilson's higher realism, a diplomatic code. First off, he was more concerned with long-term goals based on ethical standards culminating in a unique American purpose: service to all peoples. He scorned raw force as a means of achieving peace, but appreciated the place of balance of power as a realistic element in foreign policy. Should war become necessary it was to be carefully monitored and never thought of as glorious. *Dulce et decorum est pro patria mori* never figured in Wilson's realism. Yet as the crises followed in quick succession Wilson focused on the end, never allowing the means to become the end, namely, the destruction of the German nation-state however much it became a focal point of American or Allied hatred.[9]

Three distinct but closely related diplomatic dilemmas faced Wilson in 1915–16. Their cumulative effect on his decisions regarding war and peace brought him to espouse his version of a league of nations openly. It became, almost at once, a proposal challenging the method whereby peace was to reign, which hitherto had been the preserve of the League To Enforce Peace. How to respond to the sinking of the *Lusitania*, what to do about the British uses of the blockade and the blacklist, and how to react to the House-Grey memorandum? Wilson's answers to these questions were to convince him that there was too little difference between the war aims of the two belligerent alliances, and therefore the chances for an ordered postwar world irrespective of which side came out victorious were slim to none. In a certain way this assessment freed up Wilson to press his formula in his own name but more importantly in the name of the United States and, if you will, the world. By the end of 1916 and the presidential election, he would define his position in such a way—a nation too proud to fight—and retain office by a narrow margin. This victory at home tended to strengthen him in the eyes of leaders in London, Paris, and Berlin. And Wilson was fully prepared to use this to his advantage. As early as January, 1917, he announced his conviction that the war must end on the principle, made practical because of wartime conditions, of peace without victory. It was a proposition neither side was prepared to accept and so the slaughter continued.

The *Lusitania* disaster faced the president with his first dilemma: how to respond to the German government in the name of the American people? The overall loss of life was staggering but it was the 127 Americans who went down with the ship that demanded Washington address the personal as well as the diplomatic issues involved with Berlin. In the days immediately after 8 May a number of voices were heard demanding the United States join Great Britain and France in the war against the Hun. The war of words against Germany as the enemy of civilization began almost at once, with ex-president Theodore Roosevelt urging in the most extreme kind of invective condign satisfaction in the name of those who had died. Then there was the matter of neutral rights, supposedly provided for by international law and custom. This issue was complicated by the fact the *Lusitania* was to the Germans an enemy ship, flying an enemy flag and carrying some munitions that would eventually find their way to the Western Front. Nonetheless the moral indignation abroad in the land was substantial but it was not prepared to follow Roosevelt and his cadre of interventionists. The very opposite state of mind prevailed. Outrage, yes; involvement, no. Furthermore, the British were not entirely blameless: in the eyes of some; they had used civilians as a shield against the possible submarine attack, and who had been warned of the danger of embarking on any liner headed into the war zone.

The burden of responsibility remained on German shoulders as far as Wilson and his cabinet were concerned. Secretary of State William Jennings Bryan, a man opposed to war, almost as a given, argued that American citizens should be strongly advised to avoid entering the war zone on any vessel irrespective of its registry. Others in the cabinet, sharing Wilson's condemnation of the sinking, warned against an overreaction, fearful it could lead to a break in diplomatic relations between the two countries. And Wilson himself did not want to give the impression that he was ready to favor openly one side in the war by going all-out in his castigation of the other. With all these considerations in mind Wilson wrote the initial draft of the first (of three) notes to the German government, outlining the position of the United States. At the State Department, Counselor Robert Lansing sought to modify the phrase "unarmed merchantmen" to "unresisting merchantmen" but Wilson prevailed. In other words it was President Wilson who was speaking and not the Department of State. The most striking principle advanced in this first note was that of "strict accountability." The United States would hold the German government ultimately and finally responsible for such actions taken in violation of justice and humanity. These included any American ship damaged or destroyed or loss of life for any American citizen even if traveling on the ship of a belligerent if the submarine involved shot on sight. As Wilson was to reiterate, such action violated justice and humanity. Despite the almost truculent tone of the note in the final analysis it appealed to a principle devoutly believed in by the president: international morality. And of importance to the president the contents of the note, when made public, received overwhelming approval from press and people.[10]

German reaction to the note was based on national pride in the exploits of its submarine commanders as well as the central role all-out submarine warfare had in the country's grand strategy. At the same time officials in Berlin were anxious to keep the United States neutral, fearful that as the sinkings by its underwater fleet mounted

American public opinion would swing decisively in favor of war. Such an event, it was appreciated, would greatly reduce the prospect of a German victory. The official Berlin response heartened Wilson because it was made to sound like agreement with the president's humanitarian concern. At the same time Berlin expressed German distress that munitions and possibly Canadian soldiers were being transported on a passenger liner. The American government was urged to investigate and likely verify the facts. At this stage in the diplomatic maneuvering the State Department termed the German reply tendentious and evasive.

Accordingly, a second *Lusitania* Note was on its way to Berlin. The main thrust here was that "principles of humanity" outweighed mere details, including the presence of contraband or Canadian troops. Wilson went on to demand that the sinking of neutral ships and/or merchantmen of belligerents be exempted from attack under orders from the German admiralty. The term "strict accountability" resonated throughout the document, enough so that Secretary of State Bryan was moved to resign in protest. Bryan was sure that Wilson's peremptory tone was a dangerous step in the direction of war. This he could not countenance. It was a month to the day that the *Lusitania* was lost. Receipt of this second note prompted a struggle within the German high command between the hardliners and those who urged some kind of an accommodation to the American position. Whether justified by the differences among the German leaders or not, the delay was seen in Washington as a stalling for time, the Germans hoping that verbal assurances would persuade the president of German goodwill. It did not, as borne out in still a third note of protest, delivered in mid-July by Ambassador Gerard. Wilson was now in an accusatory frame of mind, indicting the German government for exempting itself from the obligation to observe principles of sea law openly endorsed in the past. Rejected was the German proposal that Washington take up with London abuses of neutral trade on the part of the British. Wilson in fact went on the attack: "In view of the admission of illegality on the part of the Imperial Government when it pleaded the right of retaliation in defense of its acts . . . the Government of the United States can not believe the Imperial Government will longer refrain from disavowing the wanton act of its naval commander in sinking the *Lusitania* . . ."[11] The note was treated in Berlin as a threat of war.

Woodrow Wilson's policy regarding the *Lusitania* crisis brought into sharp relief the inner meaning of the higher realism as a guide to understanding his diplomacy. The realism of his outlook was made clear by the second Lusitania note, bringing into play as it did a contest between a Bryanite and a Wilsonian response to the issues involved. Freedom of the seas was a long held American principle, dating from very early in the nineteenth century. Whereas Bryan was ready to concede this principle in order to avoid confrontation with Germany Wilson insisted there were boundaries that could not be breached. Bryan's idealism, if not quite a case of turning the other cheek, yielded principle to accommodation, the least line of resistance. Wilson, unwilling to proceed in that fashion, foresaw ever multiplying difficulties with German submarine warfare if it were not contained early on. When war came in 1917 it was in fact the submarine menace that promoted the chain of events leading in that direction. It must be kept in mind Wilson's purpose in 1915 was defined by the higher ground morality which, from the start, rested on justice and humanity, not legalism or realpolitik, for holding Germany strictly accountable. In his own way Wilson was a warrior, that is, he was ready to stand firm for what was right, not to fall silent when wrong should be denounced. He was possessed of a clergyman's willingness to condemn sin to the point of taking up the sword of righteousness. The higher realism was then a form of realistic idealism. Not Utopian or otherworldly, it was ground on what was so in fact rather than a retreat to fancy. Woodrow Wilson has been well described not as "fundamentally a moralist . . . but a man who lived in faith . . . in meeting the complex problems of a changing nation and world."[12]

The legitimacy of naval blockade was well established in international law and practice. The Declaration of London had sought to define the limits of its tactics and application by identifying contraband by classes. This was intended to favor neutral nations by allowing certain materials to be shipped to a belligerent without interference. Neither Great Britain nor the United States had signed this 1909 protocol; however, the United States chose to use it as a guideline for its trading activities once the war had broken out. The Wilson administration requested of all belligerents to observe the provisions of the declaration. The Foreign Office rejected this American move out of hand. Part of the problem was the newer methods of enforcing a blockade given newer methods of conducting sea warfare. The

British would have been foolhardy indeed to have stationed warships off the North Sea coast of Germany; they would have been easy submarine targets especially operating so close to their home bases. The Royal Navy resorted to a "cruising blockade," its ships constantly on the move seeking to intercept any merchant ship that might be trading—directly or indirectly—with the enemy. The State Department, at Wilson's direction, insisted that Great Britain abide by the Declaration of London and the Foreign Office was equally determined to ignore both the Declaration and United States protests. A full-scale breach in relations between the two countries was out of the question but some bad blood registered on both sides.

In the United States the British ambassador, Spring Rice, managed to calm American agitation by always addressing the issues in a conciliatory fashion. His letters to the president urged patience and understanding, explaining how critical the blockade was to Britain's survival. At the same time he advised the Foreign Office, and Secretary Grey in particular, that the Americans had a point, so when there was an instance of violation it should be treated with due consideration rising out of Anglo-American friendship. All this appeared to pay off with Wilson willing to go along with what Grey pronounced as "absolutely necessary to our very existence." Wilson took cognizance of the role of Spring Rice writing him that United States accommodation to the blockade was due in part "to your fair spirit in these trying days."[13] This was in 1914. But as the strains imposed by the war grew daily and the British became more desperate Wilson would come to worry that London's no-holds-barred tactics would likely lead to interference with American neutral rights in matters of trade.

The operation of the blockade became a serious difficulty by 1916 as the noose tightened around the British Isles, leaving the government no choice but to resort to extreme measures. This, in turn, brought a rancorous American response. The stepped-up blockade was due also to the ability of the Royal Navy, for the first time, to apply maximum force and the determination of new men in the cabinet to go all out to win the war, best summed up by Lloyd George's announced intention to "fight to the finish, a knockout." A tighter blockade with more items cited as contraband, interference with the mails, and a resort to the blacklist and white list caused an uproar from the Atlantic to the Pacific. When His Majesty's Government rejected all formal protests Spring Rice warned of a growing hostility. "We are certainly invoking on our heads a great deal of indignation from a great many powerful people," he noted in one dispatch.[14] No aspect of these tactics was more fiercely resented than the blacklisting of American firms suspected of doing business with Germany through neutral countries. How did the blacklist work? The scope and effects of the policy were startling. British steamship lines refused cargoes from firms listed as trading directly or indirectly with any of the Central Powers. Steamship lines owned by neutral interests were informed if they accepted such cargoes, of contraband or enemy destination they faced the likelihood of being denied coal at British ports. Neutral banking houses must refuse loans to companies on the list and neutral merchants must decline to contract to do any business with a blacklisted company. The blacklist was applicable to domestic transactions in foreign countries as well as those located within the empire. Based on these rules Americans in the United States might be subject to the same punitive action if they were discovered dealing with any other American firms named on the blacklist. The possibilities of injury to American firms and American citizens from these arbitrary measures could bring about incalculable interruptions of their trade. The blacklist was, in a word, blackmail.

As the tensions were building Secretary of State Lansing told Colonel House: "This blacklisting order of the English is causing tremendous irritation and we will have to do something." To President Wilson it was "the last straw." He set forth his arguments very clearly to Spring Rice knowing that the ambassador would report faithfully and without exaggeration what the president was thinking and planning to do. Both Spring Rice and his French counterpart, Jules Jusserand called the blacklist a "stupid blunder."[15] Wilson in consequence began to think about asking Congress to authorize him to prohibit or restrict exports to the allies as long as the blacklist was in use. Spring Rice cabled this information to Grey as at the same time he endeavored to moderate the president's anger. He spoke of his recommendation to his government to treat each case of blacklisting on its own merits, that firms might request to be taken off the list and names would be removed as the facts warranted. To Spring Rice it was a kind of escape hatch. Wilson, it appears, was not overly impressed but Grey agreed with the ambassador's thinking. The Foreign Secretary had long held that England could not sacrifice America's friendship if it were to win the war.

It is necessary to concentrate on the president's firmly held position on the blacklist and to dismiss out of hand the contention the administration's anti-British stance was in any way derived from a desire to court the German-American vote and the Irish-American vote in the upcoming presidential election. By midsummer, 1916, Wilson was de facto his own secretary of state. On 23 July he wrote: "I may feel obliged to make it [the protest over the blacklist] as strong and formal as the one to Germany on the submarines." On 27 July: "I would probably be obliged to go to Congress and ask for retaliatory powers."[16] A month later the president authorized Lansing to prepare a joint resolution to move against the continued use of the blacklist. Within weeks Congress had acted following the president's lead.[17] If it be argued Wilson was unlikely to enforce the law nonetheless the United States ambassador to London, Walter Hines Page, recorded the following impression of their meeting of 22 September: "he [Wilson] showed a great degree of toleration for Germany, complaining of the English."[18] The whole of this controversy helped to convince Wilson all parties to the war were bent on doing whatever had to be done to gain a complete and final defeat of the enemy. Because London (and Paris) and Berlin were afflicted with tunnel vision it was to be left to the United States and to its president to remain as impartial as possible. Thus Wilson had no choice but to be the peacemaker. Nothing speaks more convincingly to this proposition than Wilson's campaign for reelection in 1916. For purely pragmatic reasons, however much they were infused with high moral purpose, the president as politician must guard against America entering the war.

Various peace initiatives came forth during the first years of the war, from Andrew Carnegie, Henry Ford, and Pope Benedict XIV but none seemed to hold the promise contained in the House-Grey memorandum of February, 1916. Only Colonel House, acting in behalf of the president of the United States, enjoyed the necessary credentials to approach governments at war with a peace proposal. It was a plan in which Woodrow Wilson would have a starring role. House had talked peace, urged settlement of dispute by compromise even before war came. It is to his credit, if not his discernment, that he continued to search for a means of peace. The climax of these efforts came in February–May, 1916, in the form of a memorandum, the text of which read as follows:

(*Confidential*)

"Colonel House told me that President Wilson was ready, on hearing from France and England that the moment was opportune, to propose that a Conference should be summoned to put an end to the war. Should the Allies accept this proposal, and should Germany refuse it, the United States would probably enter the war against Germany.

"Colonel House expressed the opinion that, if such a Conference met, it would secure peace on terms not unfavourable to the Allies; and, if it failed to secure peace, the United States would leave the Conference as a belligerent on the side of the Allies, if Germany was unreasonable. Colonel House expressed an opinion decidedly favourable to the restoration of Belgium, the transfer of Alsace and Lorraine to France, and the acquisition by Russia of an outlet to the sea, though he thought that the loss of territory incurred by Germany in one place would have to be compensated to her by concessions to her in other places outside Europe. If the Allies delayed accepting the offer of President Wilson, and if, later on, the course of the war was so unfavourable to them that the intervention of the United States would not be effective, the United States would probably disinterest themselves in Europe and look to their own protection in their own way.

"I said that I felt the statement, coming from the President of the United States, to be a matter of such importance that I must inform the Prime Minister and my colleagues; but that I could say nothing until it had received their consideration. The British Government could, under no circumstances, accept or make any proposal except in consultation and agreement with the Allies. I thought that the Cabinet would probably feel that the present situation would not justify them in approaching their Allies on this subject at the present moment; but, as Colonel House had had an intimate conversation with M. Briand and M. Jules Cambon in Paris, I should think it right to tell M. Briand privately, through the French Ambassador in London, what Colonel House had said to us; and I should, of course, whenever there was an opportunity, be ready to talk the matter over with M. Briand, if he desired it."[19]

The memorandum was an audacious move by the colonel that may well have promised more than it could deliver. But these were parlous times, the great nations of the West were threatened with self-destruction should the fighting continue to the bitter end, and America, the one Western power a nonbelligerent, might save the day. Upon the drafting of the memorandum jointly Grey agreed to consult the war cabinet but he was firm on the point that Britain could not go forward with a conference as proposed without the full consent and understanding of France. Grey was sincerely receptive to the ideas advanced in the proposal but skeptical at the same time. Failure of the Americans to come into the war after the *Lusitania* went down continued to trouble Whitehall when it came to a mere note of refusal on the part of the Germans to come to terms. They had good reason to suspect, if given the choice, the British and French would benefit and they would suffer. What House and Wilson were not prepared for was a change of heart in London. When House returned to the United States he believed, wisely or not, with the British foreign secretary committed, the peace effort would issue forth into a peace conference. With House's information and interpretation of Grey's position Wilson's idealism soared. They were keen to see the memorandum take on a life.

The initial indications of London's cooperation in the calling of a conference were not sustained. In the months following an ongoing controversy with the Wilson administration over the arming of merchantmen heated up. In seeking to disarm them so that the attacking submarine would not sink the ship without warning, the president was playing into the hands of hardliners in Whitehall. They saw armed merchantmen as essential in the sea war against Germany. In reality Grey had fallen in with House fearful that in not doing so England would be represented to the American public as unworthy of friendship. Some of the blame for this must be attributed to Colonel House. He had somehow failed to grasp that all three of the major belligerents—Britain, France, and Germany—were locked in a dance of death, that the utter destruction of the enemy would alone satisfy their national interest. And because Britain would not proceed without the participation of France and France was scornful because it did not satisfy the French passion for revenge the memorandum was doomed. Once this became clear to House he was embittered. Meanwhile, Wilson pondered his next move, which was to be his address to the League To Enforce Peace gathering in May. As has been explained he took the occasion to speak for the first time publicly about a postwar association of nations, which would include the United States. This was certainly something for the allies to think about seriously but Grey fell back on the excuse he found the proposal "premature."

With the presidential election behind him but before his second inaugural address Woodrow Wilson delivered to the Senate one of his most cogent yet accessible state papers. It might well bear the title, "A Peace that Will Win the Approval of Mankind." His remarks were pregnant with ideas, the basic ideas that one day he hoped to see as part of a final treaty bringing an end not simply to the fighting but to the tensions produced by the rivalry of nations. Logic in combination with idealism persuaded him the time had come to delineate his vision of a future world. The German use of the submarine, irrespective of the *Sussex* pledge soon to be broken, the British employment of the blockade made more dangerous still by a resort to blacklisting, and the Anglo-French rejection of the thrust of the House-Grey memorandum made it a logical move for Wilson to speak out in the name of sanity against what he found to be the insanity of the moment. If logic functioned as leverage Wilson's idealism animated the address, though at the time, January, 1917 it might have appeared to many, in both America and Europe, as impractical. In this respect it is best not to read history forward, that is, in three months the United States would be at war with Germany.

All too often Wilson's simple statement that: "first of all this must be a peace without victory" tends to fix the eye to the point of obscuring the surrounding landscape. Given the all-out effort of peoples and governments at war in a struggle that demanded total victory in light of the price already paid, Wilson's position appeared as unreal. Yet the president believed he was the one facing the realities. And he went on: "Victory would mean peace forced upon loser, a victor's terms imposed upon the vanquished. It would be accepted in humiliation, under duress, at an intolerable sacrifice, and it would leave a sting, a resentment, a bitter memory upon which the terms of peace would rest, not permanently, but only upon quicksand. Only a peace between equals can last. Only a peace, the very principle of which is equality and a common participation in a common benefit." This passage represents Wilson, the statesman, at his prophetic best. Later in this address the president advised the senators of a deeper thing than even equality. "No peace can last, or ought to last, which does not recognize and accept the principle that governments derive all their just powers from the consent of the governed, and that no right anywhere exists to hand people about from sovereignty to sovereignty as if they were property." In addition to these fundamentals of government and law Wilson advanced a number of derivative propositions including freedom of seas, reduction and limitation of naval armaments, armies reduced in size, and munitions industries regulated by governments. Finally, as though he was speaking to the senators and no one else, peace must be followed by some concert of the powers in which the United States must play an active and honorable part.[20]

In January, 1917, Wilson was determined by history past—not alone by the raging war but by attempts and failures over the centuries to internationalize peace—to map the future. Included in that future were the Fourteen Points and the Covenant of the League of Nations, the formulation of which would thereafter be the president's guarded preoccupation despite the myriad of matters that would occupy him as commander-in-chief. Only nine days after Wilson had spoken to the senate Germany resumed unrestricted submarine warfare. War followed inevitably, and disastrously for the German empire. Entry into the war altered Wilson's approach to the peace conference. Up until then the Americans were at best well intentioned outsiders who might claim a seat at the conference table. But apart from Wilson's wisdom—the question would be asked of him: How many battles did your army fight in, and how many of your men died there?—this neutral nation would have little leverage. Once in the war United States forces and finances made the difference between defeat and victory. Wilson's place at the council board negotiating a peace treaty was secure and he would be free to make the most of it. Significantly the United States was a power associated with the Allies but not bound to them. Logic had done its work, giving Idealism the long wished for opportunity to build a framework designed and dedicated to international law and order.

By any measurement the most important statement of Wilson's war aims came in his celebrated address to Congress, 8 January 1918 in which he outlined fourteen points of a program for peace. It was one thing to speak eloquently and passionately of peace without victory when his nation was not at war. It required a higher degree of civic virtue and true statesmanship to affirm in detail the means whereby peace without victory could be attained. This was the purpose behind the president's explication of the Fourteen Points, as his outline for the common good quickly became known. Wilson's proposal has been termed the "climatic event of the war"[21] and yet it was realistic as well as idealistic. The Russian revolution, unpredictable in outcome in January, 1918, meant that Russia, having suffered grievously at the hands of the Germans, must be "allowed the independent determination of her own political development and national policy" as stated in point 6. This was only one of the specific areas referred to by Wilson needing care and encouragement on the way to independence. Contrary to some observers the Fourteen Points were not really inspired by revolutionary events in Russia, or for that matter were they the opening salvo in a counterrevolutionary movement. True, Nicolai Lenin "approved of the message and thought it a potential agency for promoting peace." Eugene Debs wrote in a similar vein saying it should have "the unqualified support of everyone believing in rule by the people."[22] More significantly many in Congress saw it as "the moral turning point in the war." As revealing as such private opinion is the Fourteen Points also served as a piece of powerful propaganda, interpreted by elements in the German government as a promise of a just peace should the war be lost. In fact, on 6 October 1918 the German chancellor accepted the Fourteen Points as a basis for peace, a move leading to the armistice a month later.

As for the Points themselves the alpha and omega set the tone. The former called for open covenants openly arrived at, the supposed death knell of secret diplomacy, deemed to have been one of the causes of the war. The last point called for "a general association of nations . . . under specific covenants for the purpose of affording mutual guarantees of political independence and territorial integrity to great and small nations alike." The remaining twelve points referred to various readjustments of boundaries, self-determination in the Balkans, and freedom of the seas among other pending questions. Taken all in all Wilson's announcement engendered a fresh environment for progressive international law and the League of Nations.[23]

A heady wine may at times make the viewer see the forest while ignoring the trees. The Fourteen Points have been termed vague in places or contradictory or at variance with well established policies. In other words, they represent one man's vision, however esteemed he was and however powerful the nation he headed. But these proposals were not his government's policies, duly arrived at. Had Wilson done no more than raised high a banner that others must follow or might choose not to follow? Could he deliver? His hopes to a large extent rested on the creation of a league of nations, in which the United States would be a leading force for world peace and order. The pitfalls could be many, dangerous to the most sure of foot. Once the league was in place and only then could the work of political and economic reconstruction go forward.

The instrument setting up a league or association of nations was a logical progression from the Fourteen Points. The league was peculiarly his idea in two respects. Wilson chose the term "covenant" to identify the league constitution, thereby solemnizing it in a way that suggested a divine dimension. The second feature of the Wilson covenant was its inclusion as an integral part of the treaty which, once negotiated, would bring a formal end to World War I. All powers signatory to the treaty would be member nations of the league. Was such a decision on Wilson's part a throw of the dice or an astute, statesmanlike move? Was he motivated by his understanding of a higher realism, or a gambit on the part of a man who saw himself as a saviour? Judgments, not to mention opinions, are bound to vary and even to clash when giving answer to these questions. But reading history forward, which comes down to nothing more, or nothing less, than not knowing the outcome of Wilson's actions, denies us the luxury of second-guessing. Thus it is true that the president was the only one of the Big Five at the Paris Peace Conference who sought nothing by way of recompense or revenge for his country. What he wanted was a treaty with the league, his league, as a component with the United States as a member. It was in the working out of the provisions of the treaty that it became his league. That he took responsibility for representing it in such a way is historically honest. But he was not the only statesman to want such a league and therefore not the only one to experience disappointment when the United States rejected the Versailles Treaty with the covenant of the league as integral to it. If Wilson's messiah complex was all too real opponents took delight in playing the devil. What role William Howard Taft had in the drama of treaty ratification as it unfolded needs to be examined.

6
Cooperation, Conflict, Failure

Woodrow Wilson's bearing at the Paris Peace Conference and his fight for the Treaty of Versailles, with its salient component, the Covenant of the League of Nations, dominates this period of American history. There can be no question of this: win or lose, an outcome in keeping with his high realism or a dismissal of it. Every other major figure, whether Lodge or Borah, Root or House had no choice but to react to Wilson and his policies. In consequence, their reactions were to be minor or major in significance because Wilson, as president, occupied the high ground. In so saying it must be added that he tried to deny to his enemies even defilade from which they might try to counter his purpose. Of these reactors, William Howard Taft was assuredly one, but with a real difference. Taft was strongly pro-league, to which the leading fellow Republicans were decidedly opposed. Was the ex-president less a Republican on that account? And if so, was that in any degree relevant given the high stakes being gambled for in Paris, in the United States, and in the Senate? The objective of how to achieve and maintain world order, a cause to which both Wilson and Taft were equally dedicated, by the midterm election of 1918 reached match point. Delegates would be assembling in Paris to formalize the end of the war and no less, the beginnings of peace.[1]

Wilson occupied a commanding position. Taft, his predecessor in office with a record of favoring international accord by means of treaties of arbitration, was the most visible and the best disposed Republican on the scene. One method of assessing Taft historically is, of course, to study his reaction to Wilsonian initiatives, both minor and major in scope. It becomes necessary, however, to go beyond that mechanism. Was Taft to be a leader of a moderate Republican response to Wilson or would he fall into the trap of merely reacting to the president's moves, thereby aligning himself with the reservationists in his own party? While president, and especially in foreign policy, he had exhibited a willingness to lead. His record was indeed estimable despite the defeats he suffered at the hands of fellow Republicans in the Senate. In other words Taft knew what it was like to be hamstrung by the upper house of Congress. And later as chief justice it appeared natural to him to want to take charge in matters of judicial reform. After the White House years Taft tended to leave politics behind him although remaining a presence in party circles. To not a few observers down to 1915 he may have appeared a used-up man, the fate of most ex-presidents during the first hundred years of the republic. He reemerged to public view as president of the League To Enforce Peace with which neither Roosevelt, Lodge nor Root was to be associated. Unlike Roosevelt he had no future political ambitions, unlike Lodge he was not supercilious or self-absorbed, and unlike Root he was willing to take an unambiguous stand on international law and order. If this analysis is sound then Wilson and Taft should have been, if not could have been, partners in the peace effort. Bipartisanship had not much figured in American politics down to their time, however, whether the issue had been the Second Bank of the United States, slavery in the territories, the disputed election of 1876, or the American colonial empire acquired as a result of the Spanish-American War. Its opposite, political partisanship, in fact figured in the first step taken by President Wilson when he called for the election of a Democratic congress in the 1918 midterm elections. Despite the common purpose of Wilson and Taft to establish a league of nations by whatever name, bitter partisan politics would, in the long run, virtually doom the prospect.

Political friction between the president and the ex-president went back some years, derived in large measure from progressive domestic legislation. Wilson's efforts in this regard were impressive, to the chagrin of Republican progressives. It made the GOP slogan that any Republican was preferable to the best Democrat sound foolish indeed. And among those Wilson had upstaged Theodore Roosevelt was the most prominent and the most critical in his judgments. The presidential election of 1916, complicated by Wilson's policy of strict neutrality, found Republicans increasingly disenchanted with the president although their nominee did not bode well for a party comeback. Charles Evans Hughes was a sound public servant but he did not have much else going for him. True, it might be said he almost won in 1916 but the fact that he did not only accentuated hostility between the parties.

For Taft personally there was another bone to pick. Wilson's choice of Louis D. Brandeis for the Supreme Court quite unhinged him. The "peoples' attorney" as he was often identified faced fierce denunciation from many quarters with Taft seeking to organize the American Bar Association to oppose the nomination openly. But Wilson prevailed and Brandeis, a man Taft described as having "much power for evil" graced the court. In part the ex-president's wrath was likely fueled by remembering that during the Ballinger-Pinchot Controversy of 1910 Brandeis brought to light that he, Taft, had altered a date on a document in order to justify his decision to dismiss Pinchot from his position as chief forester. Yet in defense of Wilson he asked Taft to serve as cochairman of the War Industries Board in 1918, a request that was accepted without hesitation. And in defense of Taft, he went out of his way to put past ill-will aside when he encountered Brandeis in Washington. Their initial conversation was frank and friendly. And theirs proved to be an amicable accommodation in the long term. As chief justice, Taft came to respect Brandeis even as their jurisprudence was often at odds.[2]

The world of politics is replete with personalities and no small number of egos. Sometimes they mesh and at other times they conflict. It is rarely a case of simon-pure ideological agreement or disagreement between and among politicians. To come to the point, William Howard Taft had an active and in ways a virulent dislike for the president. During the 1916 presidential campaign and very likely bearing in mind the 1910 encounter and then the Brandeis appointment as an associate justice, Taft was moved to let his guard down on the matter of Wilson's character. Writing privately, he described Wilson as "a ruthless hypocrite . . . who had no convictions that he would not barter at once for votes."[3] Whatever his flaws of character it is hard to accept this Taftian degrination as based on anything but spite—all of which underlines how torn Taft would be when it came to endorsing Wilson's League of Nations. Party loyalty and personal animus were at war with principle, so much so that Taft suffered ongoing strain. For a long while he pleaded the case the president was determined to see through to the end; and then he seemed to desert the cause and its undergirding principles in part because it identified him too closely with a president who saw only personal enemies in the Republican camp.

Two critical political decisions, for which Wilson has been faulted by his contemporaries, and later historians and biographers, put a heavy strain on Taft-Wilson relations. The president's determination to urge the election of a Democratic Congress in the 1918 midterm elections was the first. The second, somewhat more understandable, was his exclusion of William Howard Taft from his retinue of advisors once he concluded that he himself must be in Paris to help write the peace treaty. Taft was more dismayed by the first of these moves. In any case, his reaction is secondary to Wilson's political ineptitude. As a recognized authority on American government and political history he appeared oblivious to the likelihood that the voters, in choosing representatives and senators, would be more likely persuaded by local than by international issues. Furthermore, there as the established pattern showing the party successful in the presidential election would suffer some losses in congress at midterm polling. If Wilson were willing to make an international agenda the issue, the Republicans were prepared to challenge both the "peace without victory" proclamation and the Fourteen Points as workable plans for world order. The vote of confidence that the president had sought did not materialize and worse still, the outcome of the election could be interpreted by the British and French leaders, with whom Wilson had to negotiate, as the very opposite.

Wilson might have recovered his political footing had he chosen one or more senators to join his train of advisors in Paris, and a Republican senator would have been a master stroke. If that was impossible for him to do, he could have turned to ex-President Taft, a true-blue Republican who would become a sincere advocate of a Treaty that provided for a League of Nations. Wilson and Taft, standing together in the summer of 1919, could have come as close to guaranteeing passage of the Versailles Treaty as could be imagined. Given the political turmoil, the infighting, the extremes of positions on the issues, and the personal animosities, Wilson and Taft remaining together could be found perhaps only in the realm of imagination.

On several occasions prior to the Paris Conference Taft had shown a willingness to support and cooperate with the president in his efforts to bring about a lasting peace. In July of 1916 there was some talk of Taft going to England and to France in order to discuss with

leaders there the objectives and the functions of the League To Enforce Peace. He would not undertake this mission unless he was assured by Wilson that he favored it. But the president advised against
it. For him the timing was wrong but his critics recognized his refusal
to approve the proposal as a sure sign of insisting that he and he
alone would manage the peace process. Result: a lost opportunity for
a bipartisan diplomatic offensive.[4]

In January, 1917, Taft complained that in Wilson's "Peace Without
Victory" address he had endorsed the League To Enforce Peace on
the one hand and then proceeded to undercut what the league had
been advocating since its beginnings. Wilson appeared to say that
there was no need for the military defeat of Germany whereas Taft as
president of the league had argued that a just peace depended on victory on the field of battle, a clear-cut German defeat.[5] In December of
that year the suggestion was floated that Taft go to London for the
purpose of explaining American war aims to the British government
and to do so with the blessing of the president. At the end of a long
conversation between the two Wilson said to Taft: "I think you ought
not to go . . . . (and) I would like you to make my attitude clear on this
point."[6] In March, 1918, he further discouraged conversations between representatives of the League To Enforce Peace, among whom
would be Taft and its British counterpart the League of Nations Society.[7] Shortly thereafter Taft was joined by A. Lawrence Lowell on another White House visit. It has been characterized as a "discouraging
session" inasmuch as the president was intent on disowning the "philosophy" of the League To Enforce Peace. His main objection was to
the effect that the Senate would never accept a proposition to use
force against a recalcitrant state on a majority vote of the Council of
the League. This would amount to a surrender of the war-making
powers of the Congress. In other words a different way, a Wilson way,
must be found to ensure United States participation in the proposed
association of nations.[8]

These several encounters with Taft gave the president ample occasion to size up his predecessor. He could have had no quarrel with
Taft given his record as cochairman of the War Industries Board. The
more convinced Wilson was that he was a good Republican the more
influential Taft could be in persuading Republican senators to accept
the treaty with its league component. Or does that line of argument
not presume Wilson knew what the future held when the treaty came

before the Senate for approval? On the other hand Wilson could not have known of the rapprochement between Taft and Roosevelt when it came to planning for the postwar world. Roosevelt appeared to favor the League To Enforce Peace. Certainly he would have no time for Wilson's league ideas. He was an all-out enemy of the president whom he deemed unworthy of that high office. Taft may well have acted in this matter out of party loyalty. For years he had been known as a "good Ohio man" in all things pertaining to the G.O.P. Did Taft's own deep resentment of Wilson figure in his friendly realignment with Theodore Roosevelt or was it due to personal antipathy to the "Presbyterian priest?" Very likely one emotion acted to reenforce the other. Yet Roosevelt's sincerity in expressing a willingness to support the League To Enforce Peace, thereby spiking Wilson's guns, may well have been a ploy on his part. Roosevelt was an ultranationalist and was to insist until the end of his life the United States had to go it alone. For his part Wilson was led to believe that should the ex-president be part of negotiations in Paris he would be playing the same old political game. Taft had spoken of the Fourteen Points as being too vague and indefinite to be the foundation of a structure dedicated to building a lasting peace. Wilson was wary of him as a result, moving him to say: "I would not dare take Mr. Taft. I have lost all confidence in his character."[9] In the short view it proved to be an assessment not supported by facts. Up to a point Taft would fight the good fight for the League of Nations, not because he was ever reconciled to Wilson's way of doing things but because he put the cause of international peace above party and personality. An examination of his speeches and other forms of expression, newspaper articles in particular, reveals a commitment of mind and spirit to the league concept. As he entitled one of his addresses, "League of Nations as Barrier to any Great War in the Future," so he believed. His convictions were based on the history of wars recurring from generation to generation giving rise to the fear that civilization could not survive another worldwide conflict.[10]

From the very first day after the founding of the League To Enforce Peace William Howard Taft was indefatigable in urging upon the American people and the American nation that a league of nations, call it an association, call it a society, call it what-you-will was crucial to twentieth-century mankind. Until such time as President Wilson presented his version of such an organization Taft continued to advocate those principles stated in the warrant of the League To Enforce Peace. When Wilson announced his proposal as contained in the covenant for an association of nations Taft was faced with an awkward choice. He could hardly continue to use his influence to further the prospects of the League of which he was president. He was a private citizen, without political power, however distinguished he might be. In truth, he had to react to Wilson's covenant. And he did so in two different but related ways. He advised the president regarding revisions to the original covenant, which were intended to make it more acceptable to the people and to the Senate. And he would thereby weaken the appeal of what would become a well organized and financed campaign against the Treaty with the league as integral to a treaty of peace.

Until Wilson returned from Paris with the treaty Taft felt free to take issue with those general references to an international association to be found in the Fourteen Points. As late as December, 1918, in a lengthy article appearing in the *Philadelphia Public Ledger* he sought to identify the principles of the League To Enforce Peace as part of Wilson's thinking. Wilson "has given the world reason to believe that he favored action by a league of nations to achieve results only to be brought about along the lines of the American League To Enforce Peace." He then went on to document his position by pointing to certain of the Fourteen Points, e.g., the second point, which stated "that the high seas might be closed only by international action for the enforcement of national conventions." This and other citations led Taft to assert Wilson had committed himself to the use of force "by the combined armies and navies of the members of the League." In other words, Taft argued "we cannot suppose . . . President Wilson will be content with a treaty of mere good intentions."[11] Following this newspaper article Taft took much the same stance speaking in Montclair, New Jersey, a week later. In this address he was at pains to stress there must be some provision for a league court inasmuch as disputes between league members, sure to arise, must be justiciable. "It would be impossible for this treaty to be executed unless you have a court to interpret the treaty." After a summary statement of how the treaty should look, Taft's proposals bore a strong resemblance to the League To Enforce Peace. Whereupon, he moved the question: "If the President does come home with a treaty like this, then it behooves us all to unite to support it."[12]

From these and further statements it becomes clear Taft was thinking in terms of world government, as when he wrote early in 1919, "The function of the League may be conveniently divided into the legislative, the judicial, the mediative, and the executive." Indeed, as was pointed out, the functions of the organization would likely include at a later date the codification of international law.[13] In so saying his judicial instincts were well ahead of the realities to be dealt with. Soon thereafter, adopting a much more sober tone Taft could be heard urging constructive criticism of Wilson's emerging league outline, seeking to enlist the support of Lodge and Senator Philander Knox, reminding them that as far back as 1910 Theodore Roosevelt had endorsed the league concept in broad outline. And the day after Roosevelt's death on 6 January 1919 Taft wrote a focused article, "Roosevelt's Contribution to League of Nations" for the *Philadelphia Public Ledger*, offering the judgment that "the proponents of the League To Enforce Peace may rejoice in the posthumous aid that Roosevelt gave to the League."[14] As might be imagined, this was an artfully nuanced interpretation. Perhaps Taft was paying Roosevelt back for the collusion between him and Will Hays, which bruised relations between Taft and Wilson. It must be noted the ex-president was still adhering to the principles of the League To Enforce Peace, when days later, he addressed the National Geographic Society in Washington as he laid out possible designs for the internal structure of the league.[15] He went so far in a subsequent newspaper article to fault Wilson in this regard. "The failure of the President to indicate any definite structure for the League . . . creates an uneasy suspicion that he has not thought out any plan of his own." Was Wilson then more concerned about politics and less about establishing an effective league? Apparently Taft believed such was the case when he wrote somewhat critically: Wilson's "attitude is that of one seeking a plan which will encounter no objections either in the congress in Paris or in the congress in Washington." In this respect the president would prove to have a better feel for the politics involved than did the ex-president. But Taft did get one thing right in light of Wilson's strategy when he wrote: "No reform worth having was ever put through without a fight."[16] How true that was to be.

The frequency of Taft's judgments in print and in public addresses was a sure sign of his commitment to a new way of achieving international law and order. "The League of Nations Is Here," the title of a newspaper article dated 23 January, underscored his private hope, openly voiced. His feelings were so positively expressed, his expectations that right-thinking men from both parties would come to see the necessity, and thus the wisdom, of the league fed his optimism. The great nations, France, Great Britain, Italy, Japan, and the United States would provide the leadership and a league, once in being, would in good time invite "all other responsible powers" to join.[17] Following closely was an article he called "The League's Bite." He quoted approvingly both Wilson and Lloyd George, continuing to accent his belief in the use of enforcement, and therefore being unwilling to be dependent on "merely moral aspirations and moral sanctions." The guiding principle of the League To Enforce Peace died hard for Taft.[18]

A notable shift in Taft's outlook came through sharply in an address given in Portland, Oregon, 16 February 1919, within a few days of the news reaching the United States that the enabling document for a league had been written. "The constitution is indeed wider in the scope of its purpose than was the platform of the League To Enforce Peace . . . It is to organize a real and permanent league." From there Taft delivered a truly eloquent explanation cum defense of what Woodrow Wilson, as chairman of the conference committee, proposed for a postwar organization designed to promote peace and prevent war. Not the least of Taft's satisfaction was due to an implied proposal for a permanent international court of justice.[19] The ex-president's next stop was San Francisco where he spoke to the Commonwealth Club. Again his remarks painted a rosy picture. "I wish you would study that Covenant. I wish you would work out what it means. It is a well conceived plan. It does not involve as much compulsory force as our League to Enforce Peace has recommended, but it comes very near it; and it carries with it an arrangement for amendment and for an elasticity that, as experience goes on, will enable the League to adopt other methods." Later in his speech Taft appeared to recognize that had Wilson insisted on a greater use of force the likelihood of Senate approval would have been greatly diminished.[20]

Moving on to Salt Lake City this new convert to Wilson's League proposal warmed to his subject. But allow Taft to speak for himself.

> Some say: "Let them have a league of European nations and leave the United States out." That is a great mistake. Who would constitute such a league? England, France and Italy—three nations. You

would have an Entente Alliance; that is all—a balance of power with all the disappointing results that we have had in previous balances of power. The United States is indispensable to make that league go as a general league of nations, for the reason that it is the most disinterested member, the purest type of democracy, and its presence in the League will repudiate and refute any suggestion that it is an intrigue for autocratic action. Our presence will give to the League a potential strength and prestige which it will not have without us. So it is our duty to join, if we want to see the thing through, if we want to be square with those who fought this war for three years for us.

He also took the occasion to dismiss as fatuous the contention the covenant endangered the operation of the Monroe Doctrine and spoke directly to the issue of constitutionality raised by Article X. "It is a mistake to suppose that [under league sponsorship] armies of the United States are to be called to distant countries." But Taft, "the man of peace," saved his most empassioned appeal to endorse the higher realism of Woodrow Wilson to the last.

I appeal to the women who hear me: Do they want war again? Are they not willing that we should make concessions now in order that we may avoid war ten and twenty years hence? Do they wish their children and their grandchildren subjected to the suffering that we have seen England and France and Italy undergo? If not this the time when enduring peace is to be born—when everybody is impressed with the dreadful character of war, and the necessity for avoiding it, when all the nations are willing to make concessions? Isn't now the time to take our share of the responsibility and say to our brothers: "We realize that the sea no longer separates us but is become a bond of union. We know that if a war comes to you, our neighbor, it will come to us, and we are ready to stand with you in order to keep off that scourge of nations. In the love of our brother we will do our share as men and women conscious of the responsibility to help along mankind, a responsibility which God has given this nation in giving it great power."[21]

He had, literally, pulled out all the stops.

At the National Congress of a League of Nations in St. Louis Taft brought his western tour to an end with an address summing up his whole purpose: "League of Nations as Barrier to any Great War in the Future." He began by advancing the proposition that "the practical working of this covenant will be to suppress and avoid most wars." Well aware of rumblings that league membership would undermine the sovereignty of nations, something Americans were especially suspicious of, Taft went straight to the point. His reasoning is so comprehensive and his arguments so sustained interpretive paraphrase can scarcely do him justice.

> This covenant does not create a super-sovereignty—it is only a loose obligation among the nations of the world by which they agree to unite together in a policy of submitting their differences to arbitration and mediation, to withhold war until those efforts have proved unsuccessful and to boycott any nation which violates the covenant to comply with this obligation. It provides a method for reaching an agreement as to a limit of armament and an obligation to keep within that limit of armament until conditions shall require a change by a new agreement. The agreement on the part of one balances the agreement on the part of others in securing a general reduction of armament. It does not impair our just sovereignty in the slightest—it is only an arrangement for the maintenance of our sovereignty within its proper limits: to wit, a sovereignty regulated by international law and international morality and international justice, with a somewhat rude machinery created by the agreement of nations to prevent one sovereignty from being used to impose its unjust will on other sovereignties. Certainly we, with our national ideals, can have no desire to secure any greater sovereignty than this.
>
> The argument that to enter this covenant is a departure from the time-honored policy of avoiding entangling alliances with Europe is an argument that is blind to the changed circumstances in our present situation. The war itself ended that policy. *Res ipsa loquitur.* We attempted to carry it out. We stayed out of the war three years when we ought to have been in it, as we now see.
>
> We were driven into it because, with the dependence of all the world upon our resources of food, raw material and manufacture, with our closeness, under modern conditions of transportation and communication, to Europe, it was impossible for us to maintain the theory of an isolation that did not in fact exist. It will be equally impossible for us to keep out of another general European war. We are, therefore, just as much interested in stopping such a war as if we were in Europe. This war was our war. The settlement of the war is our settlement. The maintenance of the terms of that settlement is our business, as it is the business of the other nations. To say that we should avoid it is to say that we should be recreant to our duty to our-

selves and to the world and blind to the progress of events. To say
that it mixes us up with kings is amusing when we consider the dominance of democracy in Europe.[22]

In reading this passage today one must be struck by Taft's recognition of global realities and more particularly by the prediction that it
would be impossible for the United States to remain uncommitted in
the face of another European war.

Taft was slowly coming round to find that, in Paris, Wilson had
achieved considerable success. After all, he had endorsed the president's decision to attend the Peace Conference in person. As he was
to write for publication Wilson's presence would "stamp upon it a
democratic character in the eyes of all but the wild-eyed bolsheviki."
That "the human touch of it all" could only contribute to a better understanding of the United States position, that Wilson would be a
"most fitting head of state."[23] Considering the bad blood between
them these were more than generous words; appearing as they did in
the public prints the president could not have remained ignorant of
them. And it is tempting to think if Taft had been president he would
have done much the same thing. There are other reasons to conclude
the breach between the two men was lessening. In early February
Wilson was informed that on the recommendation of Taft, acting in
the name of 3500 delegates of the League To Enforce Peace, a cable
be sent the president in Paris announcing they would "stand by and
uphold the President in his efforts" to win an agreement to secure
the peace.[24] About the same time, 10 February A. Lawrence Lowell
and Taft cabled Wilson: "we earnestly hope before you complete the
structure of the league finally and make it public you will return to
the United States and yourself consult public opinion."[25] Lowell and
Taft were especially concerned about costs and the commitment of a
military force to maintain the authority of the league. In reply Wilson
expressed his "warmest thanks" for "very great and valuable reassur-
ances."[26] Colonel House, recognizing the value of such support,
urged the president to bring Lowell and Taft to the White House,
once he was back from Paris.[27] Changing circumstances combining
with their common cause appeared to be drawing Taft and Wilson together. Not that they were in complete agreement: they differed, for
example, on what issues coming up in league affairs were justiciable,
and what were not.

On the last day of February Wilson telegraphed Taft: "I am very glad to learn that you are to speak with me at the meeting in New York next Tuesday."[28] To which Taft replied: "I thank you for your kind telegram. I am glad to have the opportunity of emphasizing the transcendental importance and the non-partisan character of the issues in respect to the proposed League of Nations by speaking with you in New York."[29] All of this points to nothing less than a meeting of minds, at the beginning of the fight for the league.

The place, the Metropolitan Opera House in New York City, the date, 4 March 1919, on stage, William Howard Taft and Woodrow Wilson. They had come together to explain and promote acceptance of the Covenant of the League of Nations. It was a dramatic occasion featuring the most respected Republican leader of the day (recall, Theodore Roosevelt had died two months before) and the president of the United States, as the head of the Democratic Party. Both men endorsed the Treaty of Versailles, contending the league covenant was integral to it. The symbolism of their dual, complementary appearance is hard to disguise. Personal animosities and misunderstandings had been put aside as they joined in a cause in which they fully believed. Equally important was the potential for success in this historic moment. How could the Republicans turn their backs on Taft and decry his leadership? With Roosevelt out of the picture it is not too far-fetched that the Ohioan might actively have considered seeking the Republican party presidential nomination in 1920. Newton D. Baker made that point in a note to President Wilson.[30] Given the fact Wilson would be *hor de combat* and looking to the fact Governor Cox of Ohio proved to be the Democratic choice, the G.O.P. might have turned to Taft. He had failed to get his arbitration treaties with France and Britain approved in 1911, now he might be vindicated. Faced by senatorial delays designed to prevent American membership in the league his strong sense of public service could have persuaded him. That he did not seek the nomination may well have doomed the treaty and the league, the best efforts of Woodrow Wilson not withstanding. But, to get back to 4 March 1919, by placing principle above all else Taft and Wilson with reasoned explanation and emotional exhortation appealed to the American people to seize the moment when the future stood at a crossroads. It was not a perfect document, a panacea they defended, but one that once in place would be able to respond positively to crises between and among nations through league agencies for arbitration and mediation.

Taft spoke first and made the following arguments. The league would work for a reduction of armaments by all nations. Nations would have the means and the incentives to settle disputes by negotiation or arbitration before a league tribunal. From arbitration the issue in question would move to mediation as a last step before enforcement. Although the machinery for these processes had not been fully developed the league as it was first composed was "a substantial step forward" in the peaceful settlement of international differences. Any members that resorted to war, or warlike actions would be faced with coordinated official and personal pressure to cease and desist, after which could follow commercial, financial, or other forms of boycott. In such moves the Congress of the United States by law or joint resolution would have to approve American participation. Expenses involved in such measures would be shared. Without American participation in the league the powers of the world would fall back into that system of alliances and balance of power thinking that precipitated the Great War. Taft closed his remarks with the most earnest of appeals. "The League Covenant should be in the Treaty of Peace. It is indispensable if the war is to accomplish the declared purpose of this nation and of the world and if it is to bring the promised benefit to mankind. We know the President believes this and will insist upon including the Covenant. Our profound sympathy in his purpose and our prayers for his success should go with him in his great mission."[31]

Wilson spoke at less length but with equal purpose. He voiced approval of Taft's "clear and admirable an exposition of many of the main features of the proposed covenant" and he "has set a picture for you of what failure of this great purpose would mean." Wilson wanted to expand on certain matters that had not been stressed. Among these were the equality of nations, large and small alike. There must be self-determination of peoples and he pointed in particular to the subject races of the Austro-Hungarian and Ottoman empires. Subjugation of these and other ethnic enclaves could no longer be tolerated. But political independence must combine with economic cooperation. Our "boys have fought for such principles and objectives and we must act to see what they fought for will be achieved." "They went over there not to glorify America but to serve their fellow men."

Meeting the argument it would be dangerous for America to help the world. Wilson replied: "it would be fatal to us not to help it . . ."[32]

Both public commentary and private correspondence show Taft continuing to speak out in favor of the League of Nations until the summer of 1919. It was also a time period when he felt free and confident of his quasi-official relationship with the president to offer advice on treaty revisions always with an eye to ratification by the Senate in the name of the American people. A major address to the Economic Club of New York, just days after the Metropolitan Opera speech, gave him the opportunity to attack Senator Knox's so-called indictment of the league. It sounded like a lawyer's brief although there were passages of excoriation as, for example, "the whole structure of Knox's indictment falls," or "I submit in all fairness that there was never a more palpable *non sequitur* than this." What in particular had Taft singled out for his scornful attention? The power of the executive council of the league (it had no executive power), the league's war-making power (it could only recommend action, and recommendation is not declaration), nations were bound to act in military concert (each nation interpreted the meaning of the covenant), there is no supreme court (because the covenant is not a constitution), the war-making power, for the United States, was located not in Geneva (but in Washington). Taft's counterindictment was a damning one.[33]

During these weeks Taft was also busy advising Wilson as to changes in the covenant, which he believed would disarm critics in and out of the Senate. The following message, cabled to Wilson in Paris speaks to Taft's major worry.

[Washington] 18 March 1919.

"If you bring back the treaty with the League of Nations in it, make more specific reservation of the Monroe Doctrine, fix a term for the duration of the League and the limit of armament, require expressly unanimity of action in Executive Council and Body of Delegates, and add to Article XV a provision that where the Executive Council of the Body of Delegates finds the difference to grow out of an exclusively domestic policy, it shall recommend no settlement, the ground will be completely cut from under the opponents of the League in the Senate. Addition to Article XV will answer objection as to Japanese immigration as well as tariffs under Article XXI. Reservation of the Monroe Doctrine might be as follows:

Any American State or States may protect the integrity of American territory and the independence of the government whose territory it is, whether a member of the League or not, and may, in the interests of American peace, object to and prevent the further transfer of American territory or sovereignty to any European or non-American power.

Monroe Doctrine reservation alone would probably carry the treaty but others would make it certain.

—Wm. H. Taft."[34]

Taft was not satisfied that a mere listing of proposed alterations was sufficient to the need. Three days later he dispatched a long memorandum for the president's consideration. It featured not only new wording but a detailed explanation of the suggested changes. An example of Taft's method speaks not only to the ex-president's legal mind but equally so to his earnestness of purpose. The example takes up the highly controversial Article X, involving as it did the possible use of force by member states to avoid wars and thereby keep the peace.

Article X

The Members of the League undertake to respect and preserve as against external aggression to territorial integrity and existing political independence of all Members of the League. In case of any such aggression or in case of any threat or danger of such aggression the Council shall advise upon the means by which this obligation shall be fulfilled.

Taft's suggestions were detailed as follows:

Add to Article X.

(a) "A state or states of America, a member or members of the League, and competent to fulfill this obligation in respect to American territory or independence, may, in event of the aggression actual or threatened, expressly assume the obligation and relieve the European or non-American members of the League from it until they shall be advised by such American state or states of the need for their aid."

(b) "Any such American state or states may protect the integrity of any American territory and the sovereignty of the government whose territory it is, whether a member of the League or not, and may, in the interest of American peace, object to and prevent the further transfer of American territory or sovereignty to any European or non-American power."

Explanation

Objection has been made that under Article X, European governments would come to America with force and be concerned in matters from which heretofore the United States has excluded them. This is not true, because Spain fought Chile, in Seward's time, without objection from the United States, and also Germany and England instituted a blockade against Venezuela in Roosevelt's time. This fear could be removed, however, by the first of the above paragraphs.

Paragraph (b) is the Monroe Doctrine pure and simple. I forwarded this in my first memorandum.

It will be observed that Article X only covers the integrity and independence of members of the League. There may be some American countries, which are not sufficiently responsible to make it wise to invite them into the League. This second paragraph covers them. The expression "European or non-American" is inserted for the purpose of indicating that Great Britain, though it has American dominion, is not to acquire further territory or sovereignty.[35]

Plainly, Taft was seeking substantial additions be made as much out of political expediency as out of principle.

In Paris opposition developed to Wilson's proposals, altering what was intended to be the final version of the treaty and the covenant. News of this moved Taft and Lowell to cable the president again. "Republican Senators will certainly defeat ratification of treaty because public opinion will sustain this. With such amendments treaty will be promptly ratified."[36] Two days later Wilson was advised that thirty members of the executive committee of the League To Enforce Peace also feared that without the amendments the treaty was doomed. The President gratefully acknowledged Taft's advice, expressing the hope it would prove useful. His recommendations were incorporated in the final version of the covenant. And Taft was greatly pleased.

Meanwhile Taft continued to defend, explain, and promote the cause of the league. His message to people in Atlanta, Georgia was simple: the league was needed "To Make Peace Secure," the title he gave his address there. It was a short but pithy series of remarks focusing on the Monroe Doctrine and its exceptional character in the history of international law. He likened the purpose of the league to keep world peace to the role of policeman in the western hemisphere as played by the United States.[37] But it was chiefly in the columns of the *Philadelphia Public Ledger* that Taft elaborated reasons why the league should be established.

In one article, dated 29 March Taft argued against the assertion that preoccupation with the league delayed a final peace settlement with Germany and its allies. By establishing the league forthwith the various issues bound up in the full treaty could be worked out under League auspices. Conclusion: this would quicken rather than delay the final settlement.[38] Much the same point was made a week or so later in "Round Robin," not so much a denunciation of the senatorial cabal to kill the treaty aborning but to expose the illogicality of it. "Open Door Diplomacy Slow" Taft looked upon as an exercise in educating the public about the deliberate pace of diplomacy, far more likely to produce lasting results than a "quick fix." And the more so because modern day diplomacy should include input from the public in a variety of forms: news reports, editorial commentary, and town hall meetings.[39] Taft wrote disapprovingly of the secret treaties of yesteryear, one of which guaranteed Fiume to Italy after the war that had come back to haunt the peacemakers of 1919.[40] Undoubtedly the most ambitious of these newspaper writings was "An Analysis of the League Covenant as Amended." It consisted in a careful review of all the major issues brought up in response to early versions of the enabling document and how the changes made it a more understandable and therefore more acceptable from an American viewpoint. Taft noted all the provisions that had not been carefully drawn up. It was a painstaking approach aimed at the better educated of the citizenry.[41]

It would be too much to claim that Taft and Wilson had achieved a personal reconciliation as a result of this fruitful exchange of ideas, and of hopes it must be added, for the future peace of the world. Taft continued to dislike Wilson, the person. And he has left a record of his feelings. Perhaps it was no more than a matter of differing personalities, Taft more easily provoked into expressing his likes and dislikes. Wilson, in contrast, was restrained, seemingly always serious, especially when being condemnatory. As long as they agreed that the Covenant of the League must be ratified, they got along. But as it became evident that Wilson might have to make some concessions, willing to accept some of the Lodge reservations to the treaty,

Taft's position began to undergo change. And once Wilson indicated he would not accept any such qualifications to the covenant their working partnership dissolved. Beneath this surface disagreement ran deep and corrosive waters churned by personal feelings bordering on hatred, party politics undergirded by old time loyalties, and unwillingness to compromise born of quasi-ideological commitments of long standing.

Woodrow Wilson, coming home from Paris with treaty in hand, took center stage. It now became his responsibility to convince the Senate and the people that it was in the best interest of America and of the world to ratify the decisions agreed to by the Allies and to move to the task of reconstruction. Taft saw the situation for what it was. He had taken the opportunity—really, he had made the opportunity—to advise the president and had succeeded to a considerable degree. This was readily apparent, for example, in Article XXI, which read: "nothing in the Covenant shall be deemed to effect . . . regional understandings like the Monroe Doctrine for securing the maintenance of peace." In early June Taft, the leading Republican, if not the Republican leader, remained opposed to the partisan tactics of Lodge and Borah. Speaking to the Albany Chamber of Commerce 7 June he said the league belonged not to Woodrow Wilson but to the world, adding: "I don't care who gets credit for the League of Nations if it goes through."[42] That evening he expanded on this proposition at a meeting of the League To Enforce Peace in New York City. "We should be for or against the League without regard to whether we think it will bring credit to our party or to any man. Personal or partisan considerations of this kind are reasons which should have no influence with us in determining an issue so fateful to the world's history and so likely to affect the future welfare of the people of the United States and of all mankind. When therefore you come to consider whether you are in favor of the treaty or not, you should search your hearts and your souls and your consciences to see whether you are approaching it in the proper patriotic and humane spirit, or whether you are against it because Mr. Wilson is for it and you may fear that he will gain credit for its adoption, or because you may suppose that his party may gain credit for it. These are small reasons for supporting or opposing the League."[43] Under the circumstances of time and place this was a resounding endorsement of nonpartisanship. Surely Taft's words would impact on a sufficient number of Republican senators and/or their constituents to support ratification of the treaty and the league, making them the law of the land.

In the whole matter of the league had Taft taken into sufficient account the machinations of Lodge, the bile of Borah or the shiftiness of Root? Lodge was prepared to manufacture as many reservations as might be needed to defeat what he judged to be "Wilson's League." Borah went for the jugular as a matter of instinct and deliberation combined. And Root played the sly fox. He proposed the United States enter the league on its own terms, that is, however the incumbent administration would choose to interpret the covenant. Taft was thunderstruck by Root's maneuver. More importantly he was deeply worried that what seemed a few weeks before to be a certainty of ratification now faced either rejection or an emasculation so drastic as to reduce American participation in league affairs to a parody.

What to do? Taft decided that inasmuch as he could not defeat the reservationists, he would join them. But his purpose was not to defeat the treaty but to slip it past its opponents. This was a dangerous tactic and a sure sign of desperation verging on despair. In what appears to have been an offhanded way he mentioned to Arthur H. Vanderburg, then the young editor of the *Grand Rapids* (Michigan) *Herald,* that some reservations might at the end of the day become necessary to save the covenant.[44] It is not likely that he was sharing his deepest thoughts with an unknown political youngster like Vanderburg, but it does indicate that by mid-July he was thinking along these lines. In making the moves that followed Taft's behavior has been variously characterized as ingenuous and trusting, well intentioned and pragmatic, foolish and wise. Very possibly he was all of the above, which became evident as the plot [*sic*] unfolded. Will Hays, chairman of the Republican National Committee, had picked up on Taft's talk with Vanderburg, decided to exploit the opportunity it seemed to present when Taft approached him regarding the need for Taft-inspired and Taft-phrased reservations to protect the league. He continued to believe that as a Republican ex-president he could still influence the outcome in the fight for the treaty. He chose to put in writing a set of proposed amendments. For example, Taft included in his letter to Hays the following suggestions by way of reservations.

> 1. Provision is made for retirement from the League on two years notice without reservation that retirement shall be upon conditions

that the United States has fulfilled all its obligations as a member of the league, this question of fulfillment to be determined by the council. The nation withdraws as a member and the question of damages arising out of any failure to fulfill its international obligations, while a member of the league, will be determined by the machinery set up for that purpose.

2. Self-governed colonies cannot ever be represented on the council, if the home government is represented or be included in any of those clauses where the parties to the dispute are excluded from its settlement.

3. Functioning of the council under Article X shall be advisory only and not binding on the members, each of whom shall be free to determine his own obligation which in the case of the United States, would be determined by Congress.

4. Differences between the nations regarding immigration or the tariff are domestic questions and are not to be submitted to the league.

5. The Monroe Doctrine is defined as a convention under international law applicable to this hemisphere, and the right of the United States shall not be challenged in objecting to or preventing any attempt by a non-American nation contravening the principle of the Monroe Doctrine.

6. Without a waiver of any rights on the part of the United States to withdraw from the league at an earlier date, the United States gives notice of withdrawal in ten years.[45]

Hays took advantage of Taft's trusting nature by agreeing not to disclose notes he had composed and then proceeded to share them with Root. Taft's proposals were soon in newspapers favorable to the reservationists. For Taft this produced results that were doubly unfortunate. He was made to appear as joining the very Republicans he had been battling against, or to put it another way, deserting the cause of the League, in a word, a turncoat.[46] He was also viewed as having abandoned the League To Enforce Peace, which had taken a firm stand for the covenant without any reservations, unconditional ratification. Here was the president of the league that he had helped to found breaking faith. His offer to resign the presidency simply split the league and neutralized it as a force as the fight over the treaty wore on. It had become house divided against itself.

Wilson's decision to go to the people across the country, insisting in uncompromising terms the treaty be ratified as he had laid it before the Senate irked Taft. Wilson was playing into the hands of the hard-line reservationist in the West. "The President's attitude in not consenting to any reservations at all is an impossible one." In private his old anti-Wilson malice surfaced: "the truth is he is insisting on hogging all the authority . . . trusting no one."[47] Events, some of his own working, had painted Taft into a corner: a treaty with whatever reservations was better than no treaty at all. But Wilson was incapable of compromise.

Taft had only one card left to play. October found him making the rounds in Washington as the Senate prepared to take a climactic vote on the Treaty of Versailles. He wished with all his heart that the league, with or without reservations, would be approved by the Senate and had spoken to some Republican "mild reservationists" to that effect. But his presence was to no avail. What President Wilson had once called a "living thing" had died the death that November 19th, 1919. And Taft was among its most saddened mourners.

A postmortem followed. Examination of the circumstances surrounding the rejection of the treaty, which had been voted on three times by the Senate, only to be turned down, led Taft to believe a Republican president, if elected in 1920, might be able to breathe new life into the league. Any momentary aspirations Taft himself may have had for a return to the White House he had himself dashed by his harsh criticism of Lodge, Knox, Borah, and in fact the full array of the extreme reservationists. The party needed a compromise candidate and found him in the person of Warren G. Harding, a senator from Ohio. Taft soon learned that Harding had no interest in the league, or in much else besides, as he was utterly devoid of convictions. Campaigning against Governor James Cox, also of Ohio, and his attractive running mate, the young Franklin Roosevelt, both of whom were all-out Wilsonians, Harding dodged the league issue by being for and against it. Harding was a politician's politician willing to talk out of both sides of his mouth, a mere electioneering device. Once in office, President Harding, a creature of the Republican machine, allowed the League to fade over the horizon of normalcy. Woodrow Wilson had failed and William Howard Taft had failed. Taft's words were to be ominously prophetic: ". . . It was impossible for us to maintain the theory of an isolation that did not in fact exist. It will be equally impossible for us to keep out of another general European war."

Taft and Wilson enjoyed a common inheritance that to a considerable extent had a similar shaping influence on their outlook when it came to a world war and a world peace. Their personal experience in public affairs along with their different temperaments separated them in their judgments regarding the League of Nations. For all his conservative instincts Taft had learned and understood the need for compromise in meeting his various public responsibilities. His entire stay as civil governor of the Philippines involved a blending of meeting the needs of the people there and maintaining United States sovereignty. As Secretary of War his arrangement of the trade-off between Washington and Tokyo regarding American presence in the Philippines and Japanese presence in Korea produced the Taft-Katsura compromise. As president he urged passage of the Mann-Elkins Act as a middle ground between the railroad companies and railroad customers. In contrast, Wilson's experience, whether in academe or in government was often a matter of all or nothing. In his disagreement with Dean West over university organization he resigned the presidency of Princeton rather than share power with what he saw as his enemy, and a wrongheaded enemy at that. The New Jersey governorship and the "domestic presidency" went so smoothly Wilson appeared to combine being successful with being right, and being right with righteousness, a dangerous mixture. This was what his defeat on the issue of the league covenant was all about.

Taft and Wilson alike were men of conscience. To anyone who knew Taft he was jovial, hearty, at times diffident, and yet resilient. Wilson really had none of these characteristics in any meaningful way. Taft was his own best friend, Wilson was his own worst enemy as the two tried, and tried mightily, in the matter of the league. Had Taft not been diffident, thereby giving in to party loyalty instead of standing fast with the ratification commitment of the League To Enforce Peace, the covenant in one form or another could have become law. A Wilson less righteous (and less contemptuous of his opponents) might have saved the day. Historians, however, do well not to speculate about the might-have-beens. Allow Disreali to have the last word: "Read no history, only biography, for in biography there is life with out theory."

7
Perspectives

BEFORE LOOKING TO THE FUTURE, AND IN LIGHT OF THE PERSONAL INTER-
action of Taft and Wilson in pursuit of an ordered world, a renewed
notice of their personal characteristics and their ongoing conduct of
diplomacy can add to an understanding of "cooperation, conflict, and
failure." One or more examples comparing and contrasting style and
substance in these respects are best considered at first. The difference of personality types could not be more striking, which is not
simply to point to the jovial Taft and the stern Wilson. Utterly dedicated to the law Taft had come to accept that compromise, or half a
loaf, or yielding to the inevitable, were peculiar to life itself and hence
in politics, whether domestic or foreign in scope. Wilson, full of righteousness, was often justified in taking a stand *contra mundum*. Taft's
jocund side may have encouraged self-deprecation, a state he appeared to be in after the Senate had eviscerated arbitration treaties
intended for Great Britain and France. And Wilson's righteousness, if
sorely tested, could become self-righteousness, a hardening of the
heart rejecting compromise as odious and unworthy.

Such matters are apt concerns for the psychobiographer. The results of their probings, as far as may be possible when relying on the
written word, has provided analysis that is rarely persuasive. There is
the effort, for example, to add to an understanding of the historical
Taft by reference to his eating habits, that he found solace and escape from enduring the burdens of office by what is made to appear
near gluttony. But no relationship has been established between it
and the policies he pursued, whether in domestic or foreign affairs.[1]
Woodrow Wilson, however, appears to be a more apt subject for literary psychoanalysis. No less an authority than Sigmund Freud, assisted by William C. Bullitt, undertook such a challenge. The nub of

their study was Wilson's relationship with his father. According to the Freud-Bullitt interpretation Wilson never grew beyond identification with his father. Reverend Wilson experienced his supreme moments when he was expressing himself from the pulpit. According to this line of reasoning, just as his father was not in the habit of advising the practical means to translate pulpit principles into everyday life, so the president did not provide any really practical methods, for example, of compelling translation of the Fourteen Points into international practice. To point out the way was deemed by father and son to be sufficient; men would follow their direction because as agents of the Almighty they had spoken. What Freud-Bullitt had done was to offer tantalizing rather than convincing judgments on Wilson in history.[2]

Taft and Wilson were men of strong moral fiber, a quality more commonly associated with Wilson. But Taft could readily rise to the occasion, in words and deeds. His address, which he referred to as a sermon, to the Mormon community in Salt Lake City during his swing around the country in 1909, contained an arresting admonition to the spirit, and hence to the spirituality, of mankind. Being theologically disinclined his was a plea for the application of Christian charity in everyday life. His peroration went like this. "And so, my friends, what I am urging is less acrimony in public discussion—more charity with respect to each other as to what moves each man to do what he does do—and that you do not charge dishonesty and corruption until you have real reason for doing so. . . . It is one thing to prosecute a criminal when you have evidence and it is another thing to ascribe motives to the acts of men when you haven't any evidence and you are just relying on your imagination in respect to what you infer." In speaking to the Latter Day Saints as well as to the larger national Christian community,[3] Taft had drawn from the Bible, Proverbs, 15:1, "A soft answer turneth away wrath, but grievous words stir up anger." Wilson was, to be sure, openly theological in his private and public outlook. He entitled an address in Denver in 1911 "The Bible and Progress." To him the Bible was "the great charter of the human soul—the 'Magna Carta' of the human soul." And he went on: "The New Testament is the history of the life and the testimony of common men who rallied to the fellowship of Jesus Christ and who by their faith and preaching remade a world that was under the thrall of the Roman army." Urging his listeners to use their lives in the service of others he proclaimed: "Isn't this the lesson of our Lord and Saviour Jesus Christ?" As for the Bible and Progress, "We do not judge progress by material standards." America was not ahead of the rest of the world because she was rich but because her thoughts, ideals, and standards of judgment were found in the pages of divine revelation. "The Bible has stood at the back of progress." Reform therefore did not come from the top, but from the bottom, from the hearts and minds of believers.[4] Taft drew his thoughts and his strength from a creator whereas Wilson, good Calvinist that he was, accepted Christ as his personal savior. But in matters of practice as distinct from profession they stood on common ground, seeking to save the world from itself through a league of some kind to which the formally Christian nations in particular could subscribe and support.

While morality had a place in politics, and more particularly in diplomacy, neither man shrank from appealing to force as well as to goodwill in order to attain what was considered a defensible objective. Comparison/contrast of actions taken while each was president bears this out. Taft's dollar diplomacy in Central America amounted to attempts to achieve financial dominance in the process of which political stability would come about. In contrast Wilson's concern was first of all philosophical-political, that is, sound government. Yet during his administration there was more military intervention aimed at achieving this objective than by any other president. Where Taft mobilized American troops along the Rio Grande to keep a peaceful boundary line Wilson dispatched army units south of the Rio Grande in pursuit of his ideal of representative government and Pancho Villa, a futile gesture. The contrast also surfaces when as noted earlier dollar diplomacy was applied to China. Taft's vision of extending United States influence in that part of the world by means of heavy American investments was countered by Wilson's resolve that such a move could too readily compromise Chinese sovereignty.

As has been stated throughout this study, their contradictions and inconsistencies aside, Taft and Wilson were each, in their own particular ways, champions of international accord and cooperation. They were true believers. Taft's administration ended on a note of defeat, rejection of his arbitration proposals. Wilson began his administration with a pyrrhic victory in the name of the same cause. In principle, as war gave way to peace, they sought to formalize and in fact to

institutionalize the machinery that they deemed essential to advance
the well-being of mankind. But it was not to be.

The years 1920–21 saw the final "NO" vote on the treaty and the
league and the signing of peace treaties with the nations with whom
the United States had been at war. With the onset of a new decade the
country took its accustomed place in world affairs. But because of the
war and the debates over league membership this familiar position
spelled itself out in new ways, as at the same time it retained much of
its old look. The Monroe Doctrine was securely in place and in the
face of Japanese expansionist designs on China the principles confirmed by Taft and Root—the open door and the territorial integrity of
China—continued to figure in state department thinking. On the
other hand Harding's secretary of state, Charles Evans Hughes, initi-
ated the Washington Naval Conference in 1921, secretary of state in
the Coolidge administration, Frank Kellogg, embracing the spirit of
Locarno, joined with Briand of France in a peace pact in 1928, and
Henry L. Stimpson, under Hoover, announced the doctrine that would
bear his name, which condemned Japan's movement into Manchuria,
the vast northern portion of China. It may well be argued Stimpson's
foreign policy in this regard was in keeping with the Covenant of the
League while remaining apart from the body itself. All this added up
to conservative internationalism even as the United States was pointedly nationalistic in these world affairs. It brings to mind Elihu Root's
proposal in 1918 that the United States should reject the covenant as
a treaty obligation but promote the interests of world order by a consonant foreign policy. The irony becomes more acute by the presence
of Root among the several distinguished Americans who served on
the World Court, established under Article XIV of the league covenant.

Meanwhile the league functioned with some success in defusing
local wars. In 1920 it threatened the new state of Yugoslavia with economic sanctions, as provided in Article XVI, because of its repeated
incursions into sovereign Albanian territory, and to good effect. In
1922 the league undertook the financial rehabilitation of Austria, a
state much reduced in size and resources. The next year it facilitated
the evacuation of Corfu, which had been occupied by Italian troops.
And it was responsible for sponsoring a good many humanitarian activities as well. The league was not always successful but, not faced by

any threat of a war between the great powers, it appeared to demonstrate its useful place in world affairs.

The Washington Naval Conference, seeking as it did to rationalize a reduction of naval armaments, was completely in keeping with the purposes of the League of Nations. Navies in those days were the military equivalent of a nuclear strike force of a much later time. Therefore, restricting the size of the fleets of the major naval powers could lead to a lessening of international tensions. Secretary Hughes proposed a ten-year moratorium on capital ship construction and the scrapping of warships including those under construction. The United States would lead the way, scrapping thirty ships, amounting to 850,000 tons provided the other two leading naval powers, Great Britain and Japan, were prepared to accept a 5:5:3 ratio for their fleets in being. A problem arose and was resolved when France wanted to be included in the scheme without enjoying parity with Japan. Growing out of this arrangement was the Four Power Treaty. It provided the four nations pledged themselves to mutual respect in the Pacific by agreeing to refer to disputes between them to a conference of the four signatories to the treaty. To add to the irony of this new era of peace proclaimed, it was Henry Cabot Lodge who presented the treaty in the name of the United States. Woodrow Wilson, from his sickbed, had spoken words of peace with the gentleman from Massachusetts as his mouthpiece.

Vibrations of peace were felt in the 1920s, whatever their source. In 1925 the Locarno Pact, a treaty of mutual guarantees, was signed by France, Germany, Belgium, Poland, and Czechoslovakia. Included in the guarantees were the inviolability of existing frontiers and settlement of disputes by referral to the Council of the League of Nations. Two years later Briand approached Kellogg seeking a pledge of mutual support and understanding and after negotiations it fell to President Hoover to promulgate American partnership in this good-faith agreement. Again thoughts go back to Wilson, not in the details, but in the spirit of the brotherhood of nations.

Japanese aggression against neighboring China was an event deplored both in Geneva and in Washington and the reaction from both the league and the United States had a close commonality. Japan and China were members of the league so that this constituted the first direct clash of national interests to test the letter and the spirit of the covenant. The Council in Geneva in accordance with Article XI asked both nations to withdraw troops from the areas in dispute, and invited American participation, which was declined. When the Council appointed a special commission the United States did assign an observer to what was to be called the Lytton Commission after its chairman, Lord Lytton. The commission concluded Japan had violated the terms of the covenant and called for its withdrawal from Manchuria in accordance with its obligations as a league member. Acting independently, not in law but in common purpose, the secretary of state, enunciated the principle of nonrecognition of "the fruits of aggression." The Japanese response was to quit the league and continue its buildup on the Asian mainland. The council found itself unable to take any effective retaliatory measures. The very essence of collective security as an operable reality was thereby undermined. Subsequent military action by Italy in Ethiopia, Germany in western and eastern Europe, and the Soviet Union in Finland had reduced the league to what the more cynical termed an Anglo-French debating society.

In significant ways American foreign policy in the 1920s was in phase with the work of the league. And it experienced the same lack of will when faced with Japan's intransigent rejection of collective security. In ways this was much more a defeat for the United States. The open door and Chinese territorial integrity were positions taken by Washington as along before as 1900, and the Second Open Door Note, which had been restated in the Lansing-Ishii Agreement of 1917. As the League of Nations went into decline the United States became isolationist. If Woodrow Wilson's dream was to survive at all it would have to take on a different form. True, the driving force behind its successor organization, the United Nations, was Franklin Delano Roosevelt, a Wilsonian when the then president was pushing for American membership in the league. Franklin Delano Roosevelt was to remain an internationalist all the while and there is some evidence of Wilson's moral fervor in the Four Freedoms, as articulated by Roosevelt in 1941. The United Nations was in no way a reincarnation of the league however. It sought to achieve a more ordered world, as it would be orchestrated by the powers, assisted by a rotation of small nations in the Security Council, and it would do so by police action. All of which redirects attention to the League To Enforce Peace and ideas advanced most prominently by William Howard Taft. Undoubtedly Taft was thinking, subconsciously if you will, about major nations governing the world when he proposed arbitration treaties between the United States and Great Britain and France. He envisioned other nations, Germany, Japan, and Italy, coming together to see the wisdom of arbitration as a means of settling disputes and avoiding wars. This rationale of *weltpolitik* was a leading proposition in Warrant From History, containing as it did the foundational thinking of the League To Enforce Peace. It read in its crucial clause: ". . . we believe and solemnly urge that the time has come to devise and to create a working union of the sovereign nations to establish peace among themselves and to guarantee it by all known and available sanctions at their command, to the end that civilization may be conserved, and the progress of mankind in comfort, enlightenment and happiness may continue." The great sovereign nations were the only ones to count in world affairs in Taft's time and it was to them he had appealed for prewar treaties of arbitration. No one would argue that World War I would have been avoided by "mere" treaties, pieces of paper that is, but it may be contended that such a league of great sovereign nations, including victors and vanquished alike, might well have made a second world war unnecessary to prove the point and the principles upon which the United Nations was brought into being. In the long view the sustained efforts of Taft and Wilson, as different as their thinking was, had a shaping effect on world order throughout their century.

Notes

1. A Common Inheritance

1. Theodore Dwight Woolsey, *An Introduction to International Law* (New York: Charles Scribner's Sons, 1871), pp. 1–33. For specifics of Taft's studies, see Yale College Class Book, 1878, Yale College Records, Yale University Archives. For an overview of Taft's Yale education, see David H. Burton, *The Learned Presidency*, (Madison, NJ: Fairleigh Dickinson University Press, 1988), pp. 92–96.

2. Theodore Dwight Woolsey, *Political Science*, 2 vols. (New York: Charles Scribner's Sons, 1866), pp. 299–303. For specifics of Woolsey's influence on Wilson, see *The Papers of Woodrow Wilson*, Arthur S. Link et al editors, 69 vols. (Princeton: Princeton University Press, 1966–94), Vol. 1: p. 434, 494, 592; Vol. 2: pp. 345–47, pp. 353–54, p. 404, 409; Vol. 4: p. 134, p. 268. For an overview of Wilson's preparation at Princeton, see Henry W. Bragdon, *Woodrow Wilson The Academic Years* (Cambridge, Harvard University Press, 1967), pp. 58 ff.

3. Wesley L. Gould, *An Introduction to International Law* (New York: Harper Brothers, 1957), pp. 32–34.

4. Paul Sigmund, *St. Thomas Aquinas on Politics and Ethics* (New York: W. W. Norton, 1988).

5. Dante, *De Monarchia*, trans. Herbert Schneider (Indianapolis, IN: Bobbs-Merrill Company, 1982), p. 26, p. 16.

6. Francisco Suarez, *De Legibus*, Bk. 1, ch. 4, *The Classics of International Law*, 3 vols., James Brown Scott, ed. (Oxford: Clarendon Press, 1944), vol. 2.

7. For a sketch of Gentilis's life and work see Charles H. Stockton, *Outlines of International Law*, (New York: Charles Scribner's Sons, 1914), p. 32.

8. Grotius's place and influence are summarized in A. Nussbaum, *A Concise History of the Law of Nations* (New York: Macmillan, 1954), pp. 102–7.

9. Woolsey, *International Law*, pp. 256–57.

10. Gould, *An Introduction to International Law*, pp. 605, 619.

11. Stockton, *Outlines of International Law*, pp. 45–46.

12. For in-depth treatments of the peace movement see Merle Curti, *The American Peace Crusade 1815–1860* (Durham: Duke University Press, 1929) and Curti,

Peace or War, the American Struggle (New York: W. W. Norton Company, 1936), Chambers, John Whiteclay, ed., *The Eagle and the Dove the American Peace Movement and United States Foreign Policy 1900–1922*, (Syracuse: Syracuse University Press, 1991) is a valuable compendium of documentation.

2. TAFT IN ACTION

1. Henry F. Pringle, *The Life and Times of William Howard Taft*, 2 vols., (New York: Farrar & Rinehart, 1939) remains the richest study of Taft despite its datedness. Focusing on Taft's public life, which draws on the more recent scholarship, is David H. Burton, *William Howard Taft In The Public Service* (Melbourne, Florida: Krieger Publishing Company, 1986).

2. Garel Grunder and William P. Livezy, *The Philippines and the United States*, (Norman, University of Oklahoma Press, 1951) offers a detailed and balanced history of its subject. Chapters 1 through 9 deal with the early, difficult years of American colonialism.

3. Lewis L. Gould, *The Presidency of William McKinley* (Lawrence: University of Kansas Press, 1980) treats McKinley's thinking regarding the establishment of a stable government in the Philippines. pp. 184–87.

4. Ralph E. Minger, *William Howard Taft and American Foreign Policy, The Apprenticeship Years, 1900–1908*, (Urbana: University of Illinois Press, 1975) has the best account of Taft's response to his nomination by McKinley to take on the Philippines assignment.

5. Taft to Henry and Horace Taft, 12 Jan. 1900, Pringle, *William Howard Taft*, vol. 1, 160.

6. John Morgan Gates, *Schoolbooks and Krags, The United States Army in the Philippines, 1898–1902*, (Westport, CT: Greenwood Publishing Company, 1973) provides an in-depth account of the military operations, including the emergence of Taft in his years as civil governor as well as an assessment of the military situation as of 1900. See also, Stuart Creighton Miller, *"Benevolent Assimilation"* (New Haven: Yale University Press, 1984).

7. Taft to Charles Taft, 12 Jan. 1900, Pringle, *William Howard Taft*, 1, 185.

8. Gates, *Schoolbooks and Krags*, pp. 248–50.

9. Pringle, *William Howard Taft*, 1, discusses Taft's appointment as Secretary of War, 1, 256–62.

10. Minger, *Taft and American Foreign Policy*, p. 103.

11. Taft to Charles Taft, 17 Nov. 1904, Minger, *Taft and American Foreign Policy*, pp. 106-7.

12. Taft to Roosevelt, 15 Sept. 1906, Minger, *Taft and American Foreign Policy*, p. 124.

13. Roosevelt to Taft, 26 Sept. 1906, *Letters of Theodore Roosevelt* 8 vols. Elting E. Morison, ed. (Cambridge, Harvard University Press, 1951–54), vol. 5, 423.

14. As Roosevelt wrote to Taft: " . . . if we are not prepared to establish a strong and suitable base for our navy in the Philippines, then we had better give up the Philippines entirely." 31 May 1905, *Roosevelt Letters*, vol. 4, 1198.

15. Taft, "Japan and Her Relations With the United States," vol. I, pp. 115–19; pp. 116–17, *The Collected Works of William Howard Taft* 8 vols. David H. Burton, Editor, (Athens, Ohio: Ohio University Press, 2001).

16. Walter V. Scholes and Maria V. Scholes, *The Foreign Policies of the Taft Administration*, (Columbia, University of Missouri Press, 1970), p. 43.

17. Scholes and Scholes, *Foreign Policies*, p. 66.

18. Burton, *William Howard Taft in the Public Service*, pp. 87–88.

19. Archibald Willingham Butt, *Taft and Roosevelt: The Intimate Letters of Archie Butt*, 2 vols., (New York: Doubleday, Doran and Co., 1930), vol. 2, 635.

3. WILSON IN CONTEMPLATION

1. Wilson, "Address Before the Pennsylvania State Sabbath Association, Oct. 17, 1904." Quoted in Ray S. Baker, *Woodrow Wilson: Life and Letters,* 4 vols. (Garden City, NY: Doubleday Doran, 1925), vol. 1, p. 66–67.

2. Woodrow Wilson, *A History of the American People*, 5 vols., (New York and London: Harper and Brothers, 1901).

3. Woodrow Wilson, *Division and Reunion*, (New York and London, Longmans, Green and Company, 1893).

4. Woodrow Wilson, *The State* (Boston, D.C.: Heath & Company, 1898), pp. 85–88.

5. Woodrow Wilson, "The Study of Administration," *The Papers of Woodrow Wilson*, vol. 5, pp. 359–80.

6. Woodrow Wilson, *Wilson Papers*, vol. 5, 374.

7. Woodrow Wilson, "The Character of Democracy," *Wilson Papers*, vol. 6, 221–39.

8. Woodrow Wilson, *The State*, pp. 85–86.

9. Woodrow Wilson, *The State*, p. 86.

10. David H. Burton, *The Learned Presidency*, p. 162.

11. Wilson, *A History of the American People*, vol. 3, pp. 64–82.

12. Wilson, *Division and Reunion*, pp. 254–56.

13. Ibid., 303.

14. Wilson, *a History of the American People*, vol. 3, p. 64.

15. Ibid., 71.

16. Wilson, Public Statement, *Foreign Relations* (1913) Washington, D.C.: Government Printing Office (1920).

17. Wilson, *Wilson Papers*, 27 Oct. 1913, vol. 28, pp. 448–52.

18. Wilson, *Foreign Relations*, 13 March 1913, p. 7.

19. Wilson to Lansing, 4 Aug. 1915, quoted in Arthur S. Link, *Wilson The Struggle for Neutrality* 1914–1915, (Princeton, Princeton University Press, 1960), p. 536.

20. Link, *Wilson The Struggle for Neutrality*, pp. 512–14.

21. Wilson to Robert Lansing, 18 February 1918, *The Public Papers of Woodrow Wilson*, ed. Ray S. Baker, 8 vols., (New York: Harper & Brothers, 1925–27) vol. 7, p. 550.

22. Wilson to Sir William Tyrell, 22 Nov. 1913, quoted in Burton J. Hendrick, ed. *The Life and Letters of Walter Hines Page*, 3 vols. (Garden City, N.Y.: Doubleday Doran and Company, 1923–26) vol. 1, p. 204.

23. Wilson, Message to Congress, 20 April 1914, *Wilson Papers*, vol. 29, pp. 471–74.

24. Arthur S. Link, *Wilson The New Freedom*, (Princeton: Princeton, Princeton University Press, 1956), pp. 386–87.

25. Thomas F. Bailey, *A Diplomatic History of the American People* (New York: Appleton Century Crofts, 1951), p. 608.

26. Wilson, Statement to the Press, 2 June 1915, *Wilson Papers*, vol. 33, pp. 303–4.

4. TAFT'S REALISM

1. William Howard Taft *The United States and Peace*, (New York, Charles Scribner's & Sons,1914).

2. Ibid., p. 15.

3. Ibid., p. 29.

4. Ibid., p. 44.

5. Taft, *The United States and Peace*, p. 50.

6. Ibid., p. 76.

7. Ibid., p. 76.

8. Ibid., p. 90.

9. Taft, *The United States and Peace*, p. 94.

10. Ibid., p. 114.

11. Ibid., p. 98.

12. Ibid., p. 105.

13. Taft, *The United States and Peace*, p. 131.

14. Ibid., p. 133.

15. Ibid., p. 174.

16. Ibid., p. 180.

17. Cited in Ruhl J. Bartlett, *The League to Enforce Peace*, (Chapel Hill: University of North Carolina Press, 1944), pp. 40–41.

18. A. Lawrence Lowell, "A League to Enforce Peace," *Literary Digest*, LI, 18 September 1915, vol. 51, pp. 594–95.

19. Theodore Roosevelt, "International Peace," *The Works of Theodore Roosevelt*, Memorial Edition 24 vols. (New York: Charles Scribners' Sons, 1925) vol. 18, pp. 410–15; p. 414.

20. Philip C. Jessup, *Elihu Root*, 2 vols. (New York: Dodd, & Co., 1938) vol. 2, p. 376.

21. Henry Cabot Lodge, *War Addresses, 1914–1917*, (Boston: Houghton Mifflin Company, 1917) pp. 23–48.

22. William C. Widenor, *Henry Cabot Lodge and the Search for an American Foreign Policy* (Berkeley: University of California Press, 1980), p. 227.

23. Woodrow Wilson, *The Papers of Woodrow Wilson*, vol. 37, pp. 113–17; p. 115.

24. William Howard Taft, *Taft Papers on League of Nations*, (New York: Macmillan, 1920) pp. 28–46; p. 29. See also Taft, "Proposals of the League to Enforce Peace," p. 46–52.

25. Taft, "Constitutionality of the Proposals," *Taft Papers*, pp. 520–60.

26. Taft, "A Constructive Plan for Human Betterment," *Taft Papers*, pp. 61–74.

27. Taft, "The Purpose of the League," *Taft Papers*, pp. 74–81.

28. Taft, *World Peace*, (New York: George H. Doran & Co., 1917) pp. v–xiii.

29. Ibid., pp. 19–24.

30. Ibid., pp. 57–62; pp. 69–73.

31. Ibid., pp. 93–97.

32. Taft, *World Peace*, pp. 115–19.

5. Wilson's Higher Realism

1. Wilson, "July 4th Address," *Wilson Papers*, vol. 30, pp. 248–55; p. 254.

2. Cited in Arthur S. Link, *Wilson The Struggle For Neutrality*, p. 54.

3. Thomas J. Knock, *To End All Wars* (New York: Oxford University Press, 1920), pp. 153–54.

4. Charles Seymour, *Intimate Papers of Colonel House*, 4 vols. (Boston and New York: Houghton Mifflin Co., 1926), vol. 1, p. 264.

5. Kurt Wimer, "Woodrow Wilson and World Order," pp. 146–73; p. 148 note 12; and p. 166 in Arthur S. Link ed., *Woodrow Wilson and a Revolutionary World* (Chapel Hill: University of North Carolina Press, 1982). Alexander L. George and Juliette L. George, *Woodrow Wilson and Colonel House* (New York: Dover Publications, Inc., 1956), pp. 183–94.

6. David H. Burton, *Cecil Spring Rice A Diplomat's Life*, (Madison, New Jersey: Fairleigh Dickinson University Press, 1990), p. 152.

7. Wilson, "First Inaugural Address," *Wilson Papers*, vol. 27, pp. 148–52; pp. 151–52.

8. Wilson, Public Statement, *Foreign Relations*, 1913, p. 7.

9. Arthur S. Link, *The Higher Realism of Woodrow Wilson* (Nashville, TN: Vanderbilt University Press, 1971), pp. 127–39; p. 135.

10. The United States' position is fully set forth in the first note, 13 May 1915, *Foreign Relations*, 1915 supplement, "The World War," pp. 393–96. Subsequent notes were largely reiterations but with added emphasis.

11. Wilson, 15 July 1915, *Wilson Papers*, vol. 33, pp. 530–32.

12. Link, *The Higher Realism*, p. 139.

13. Burton, *Cecil Spring Rice: A Diplomat's Life*, p. 161.

14. Ibid., p. 184.

15. Ibid.

16. Wilson, 23 July, 27 July 1916, *Wilson Papers*, vol. 37, p. 467; p. 480.

17. Burton J. Hendrick, *The Life and Letters of Walter H. Page*, vol. 2, p. 185.

18. Seymour, *The Intimate Papers of Colonel House*, vol. 2, pp. 203–4.

19. Wilson, Address to the Senate, 22 January 1917, *Wilson Papers*, vol. 40, pp. 523–29 passim.

20. Thomas J. Knock, *To End All Wars*, p. 146.

21. Ibid., p. 146.

22. Wilson, The Fourteen Point Address to Congress, 8 January 1918, *Wilson Papers*, vol. 45, pp. 534–39; Wilson, Four Supplementary Points, Mount Vernon Address, 4 July 1918, *Wilson Papers*, vol. 48, pp. 514–17.

23. John Morton Blum, *Woodrow Wilson and the Politics of Morality* (Boston: Little Brown and Company, 1950), p. 148.

6. COOPERATION, CONFLICT, FAILURE

1. Ruth Cranston, *The Story of Wilson* (New York: Simon and Schuster, 1945) is vintage laudation of Wilson and his work. Treatment of his search for world peace is extensive and sensitive.

2. Burton, *Taft*, p. 71, pp. 131–33.

3. Knock, *To End All Wars*, p. 101, note 62.

4. Pringle, *Taft*, pp. 933–34.

5. Ibid., pp. 934.

6. Cited in Pringle, *Taft*, pp. 935.

7. Pringle, *Taft*, pp. 936.

8. Ibid., pp. 937.

9. Cited in Knock, *To End All Wars*, p. 190, note 106.

10. *Taft Papers*, pp. 257–62.

11. "President Wilson and the League of Nations," *Taft Papers*, pp. 169–72.

12. "The League: Why And How," *Taft Papers*, pp. 177–94; p. 190.

13. "Representation in the League," *Taft Papers*, pp. 195–97; p. 195.

14. "Roosevelt's Contribution to the League of Nations," *Taft Papers*, pp. 201–4.

15. "The League of Nations, What It Means and Why It Must Be," *Taft Papers*, pp. 205–10.

16. "League of Nations and President Wilson's Advisers," *Taft Papers*, pp. 210–13; p. 211.

17. "The League of Nations Is Here," *Taft Papers*, pp. 213–17.

18. "The League's Bite," *Taft Papers*, pp. 217–21; p. 219.

19. "The Great Covenant of Paris," *Taft Papers*, pp. 228–41; p. 229.

20. "To Business Men," *Taft Papers*, pp. 241–47; p. 244.

21. "Address At Salt Lake City," *Taft Papers*, pp. 249–62; p. 257.

22. "League of Nations as Barrier to any Great War In Future," *Taft Papers*, pp. 257–62.

23. Cited in Knock, *To End All Wars*, p. 191.

24. *Wilson Papers*, n.d., vol. 56, p. 37.

25. Ibid., 10 Feb. 1919, vol. 55, p. 65.

26. Ibid., 14 Feb. 1919, vol. 55, p. 187.

27. Ibid., 26 Feb. 1919, vol. 55, p. 257.

28. *Wilson Papers*, 28 Feb. 1919, vol. 55, p. 328.

29. Ibid., 1 March 1919, vol. 55, p. 357–58.

30. Newton D. Baker to Wilson, 24 July 1919, *Wilson Papers*, vol. 61, p. 614.

31. "The Paris Covenant for A League of Nations," *Taft Papers*, pp. 262–80.

32. "An Address at The Metropolitan Opera House," 4 March 1919, *Wilson Papers*, 4 March 1919, vol. 55, p. 413–421.

33. "Answer to Senator Knox's Indictment," *Taft Papers*, pp. 281–90; p. 281, p. 285.

34. Taft to Wilson, 18 March 1919, *Wilson Papers*, vol. 56, p. 83. It is this kind of support noted here that has led to the judgment that Taft was a "paragon of enlight-

enment and bipartisan harmony." John Milton Cooper, Jr., *Breaking the Heart of the World*, (Cambridge: Cambridge University Press, 2001), p. 418.

35. Taft to Wilson, 21 March 1919, *Wilson Papers*, vol. 56, p. 158.

36. 10 April 1919, *Wilson Papers*, vol. 57, p. 233.

37. "To Make Peace Secure," *Taft Papers*, pp. 295–300.

38. "League of Nations Has Not Delayed Peace," *Taft Papers*, pp. 300–303.

39. "'Open Diplomacy' Slow," *Taft Papers*, pp. 303–5.

40. "Secret Treaty Provision," *Taft Papers*, pp. 311–13.

41. "Analysis of League Covenant As Amended," *Taft Papers*, pp. 313–21.

42. Cited in Alan Cranston, *The Killing of the Peace*, (New York: Viking Press, 1945), p. 115.

43. Cited in Cranston, *The Killing of the Peace*, p. 116.

44. Cranston, *The Killing of the Peace*, p. 130–32.

45. Taft to Hays, 23 July 1919, *Wilson Papers*, vol. 61, p. 606.

46. Pringle, *Taft*, pp. 949–50.

47. Cited in Pringle, *Taft*, p. 948.

7. Perspectives

1. Some attention is given Taft's weight problem in Pringle, *William Howard Taft*, vol. 1, pp. 286–88. More sustained interest may be found in Judith I. Anderson, *William Howard Taft An Intimate History* (New York: Norton, 1981), 27–31, 125–27, 172–73.

2. Sigmund Freud & William C. Bullitt, *Thomas Woodrow Wilson: A Psychological Study* (Boston: Houghton-Mifflin Company, 1967) is a complex explanation aimed at simplifying understanding of the subject. Edwin Weinstein, *Woodrow Wilson: A Medical and Psychological Study* (Princeton: Princeton University Press, 1981) is concerned largely with ill health and its impact on Wilson's personality.

3. Taft, *The Collected Works of William Howard Taft*, vol. 3, pp. 204–10, p. 209.

4. *Wilson Papers*, vol. 23, pp. 12–20; 15, 16, 17, 18.

Bibliography

Anderson, Donald F., *William Howard Taft: A Conservative Conception of the Presidency*. Ithaca: Cornell University Press, 1968.

Anderson, Judith I., *William Howard Taft An Intimate History*. New York: Norton, 1981.

Bailey, Thomas F. *A Diplomatic History of the American People*. New York: Appleton Century Crofts, 1960.

Baker, Ray S., ed. *The Public Papers of Woodrow Wilson*, 8 vols. New York: Harper and Brothers, 1925–27.

Bartlett, Ruhl J., *The League to Enforce Peace*. Chapel Hill: University of North Carolina Press, 1944.

Blum, John M., *Woodrow Wilson and the Politics of Morality*. Boston: Little Brown and Company, 1950.

Bragdon, Henry W., *Woodrow Wilson: the Academic Years*. Cambridge: Harvard University Press, 1967.

Burton, David H., *Cecil Spring Rice A Diplomat's Life*. Madison, NJ: Fairleigh Dickinson University Press, 1990.

———. *The Learned Presidency*, Madison, N.J., Fairleigh Dickinson University Press, 1988.

———. *William Howard Taft In The Public Service*, Melbourne, Florida: Krieger Publishing Company, 1986.

Butt, Archibald W., *Taft and Roosevelt: The Intimate Letters of Archie Butt*, 2 vols. New York: Doubleday Doran, 1930.

Chambers, John W., ed. *The Eagle and the Dove*. Syracuse, NY: Syracuse University Press, 1991.

Clements, Kendrick, *Woodrow Wilson World Statesman*. Boston: Twayne, 1987.

Coletta, Paolo E., *The Presidency of William Howard Taft*. Lawrence: University of Kansas Press, 1973.

Cooper, John Milton, Jr., *Breaking the Heart of the World*. Cambridge: Cambridge University Press, 2001.

Cranston, Alan, *The Killing of the Peace*, New York: Viking Press, 1945.

137

Cranston, Ruth, *The Story of Woodrow Wilson*. New York: Simon and Schuster, 1945.

Curti, Merle, *The American Peace Crusade, 1815–1920*. Durham: Duke University Press, 1929.

———. *Peace Or War, The American Struggle*, New York: W. W. Norton Co., 1936.

Dante, *De Monarchia*, Herbert Scheinder, trans. Indianapolis, IN: Bobbs-Merrill Company, 1982.

Dougherty, James E. and Robert Pfaltzgraff, *Contending Theories of International Relations*. New York: Longman, 1996.

Dougherty, James E., *Security Through World Law and World Government: Myth or Reality?* Philadelphia: Foreign Policy Research Institute, 1974.

Duffy, Herbert S., *William Howard Taft*. New York: Minton Balch, 1930.

Ferrell, Robert H., *Woodrow Wilson and World War I, 1917–1921*. New York: Harper Row, 1985.

Freud, Sigmund and William C. Bullitt, *Thomas Woodrow Wilson: A Psychological Study*. Boston: Houghton-Mifflin Company, 1967.

Gates, John M., *Schoolbooks and Krags*. Westport, CT: Greenwood Press, 1973.

Gould, Louis L., *The Presidency of William McKinley*. Lawrence, KS: University of Kansas Press, 1988.

Gould, Wesley L., *An Introduction to International Law*. New York: Harper Brothers, 1957.

Grunder, Garl and William P. Livezy, *The Philippines and the United States*. Norman, OK: University of Oklahoma Press, 1951.

Hendrick, Burton J. ed. *The Life and Letters of Walter Hines Page*, 4 vols. Garden City: Doubleday Doran, 1923–25.

Jessup, Philip C., *Elihu Root*, 2 vols. New York: Dodd and Company, 1938.

Knock, Thomas L., *To End All Wars*. New York: Oxford University Press, 1992.

Kuehl, Warren, *Seeking World Order*. Nashville, TN: Vanderbilt University Press, 1968.

Link, Arthur S., *Wilson and the New Freedom*. Princeton: Princeton University Press, 1956.

———. *Wilson and the Struggle for Neutrality*. Princeton: Princeton University Press, 1960.

———. *The Higher Realism of Woodrow Wilson*. Nashville, TN: Vanderbilt University Press, 1971.

———. *Woodrow Wilson and a Revolutionary World*. Chapel Hill: University of North Carolina Press, 1986.

Lodge, Henry Cabot, *War Addresses 1914–1917*. Boston: Houghton Mifflin Co., 1917.

Miller, Stuart C., *"Benevolent Assimilation."* New Haven, CT: Yale University Press, 1984.

Minger, Ralph E., *William Howard Taft and American Foreign Policy: The Apprentice Years, 1900–1908*, Urbana: University of Illinois Press, 1975.

Mulder, John M., *Woodrow Wilson: The Years of Preparation*. Princeton: Princeton University Press, 1978.

Nussbaum, A., *A Concise History of the Law of Nations*. New York: MacMillan, 1954.

Pringle, Henry F., *The Life and Times of William Howard Taft*. New York: Farrar and Rinehart, 1939.

Roosevelt, Theodore, *The Works of Theodore Roosevelt*, 24 Memorial Edition, 24 volumes. New York: Charles Scribner's, 1923–26.

———. *Letters of Theodore Roosevelt*, 8 vols., Elting E. Morison, ed. Cambridge: Harvard University Press, 1951–54.

Scholes, Walter and Maria V. Scholes, *The Foreign Policy of the Taft Administration*. Columbia, MO: University of Missouri Press, 1970.

Scott, James Brown, ed. *The Classics of International Law*, 3 vols. Oxford: The Clarendon Press, 1944.

Seymour, Charles, *Intimate Papers of Colonel House*, 4 vols. Boston and New York: Houghton Mifflin, 1926.

Sigmund, Paul, *St. Thomas Aquinas on Politics and Ethics*. New York: W.W. Norton, 1988.

Stockton, Charles H., *Outline of International Law*. New York: Scribner's, 1914.

Taft, William Howard, *The United States And Peace*. New York: Scribner's 1914.

———. *Taft Papers on League of Nations*, New York, MacMillan, 1920.

———. *The Collected Works of William Howard Taft*, 8 vols. Edited by David H. Burton. Athens: Ohio University Press, 2001–4.

Thorsen, Niels A., *The Political Thought of Woodrow Wilson*. Princeton: Princeton University Press, 1988.

Walworth, Arthur, *America's Moment, 1918*. New York: Norton, 1977.

Weinstein, Edward, *Woodrow Wilson A Medical and Psychological Study*. Princeton: Princeton University Press, 1981.

Widenor, William C., *Henry Cabot Lodge and the Search for an American Foreign Policy*. Berkeley: University of California Press, 1980.

Wilson, Woodrow, *Division And Reunion*. New York and London: Longmans Green and Company, 1893.

———. *The State*. Boston: D. C. Heath & Co., 1898.

———. *A History of the American People*, 5 vols. New York: Harper Brothers, 1901.

———. *Papers of Woodrow Wilson*, 69 vols. Princeton: Princeton University Press, 1966–94.

Woolsey, Theodore Dwight, *Political Science*, 2 vols. New York: Scribner's, 1866.

———. *International Law*. New York: Charles Scribner, 1871.

Index